W9-CAH-886

What I Saw

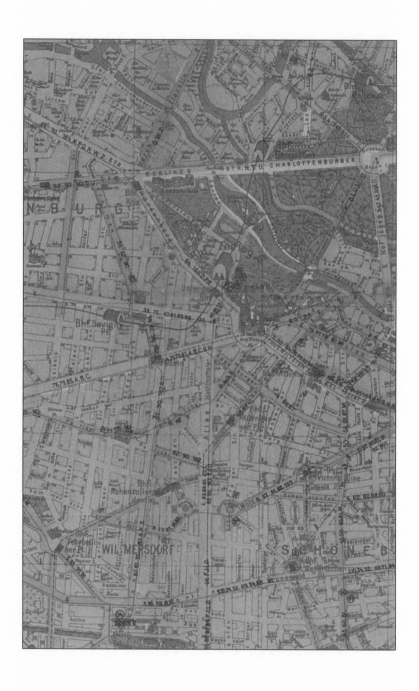

BY JOSEPH ROTH

The Collected Stories of Joseph Roth
The Wandering Jews
Rebellion
The Tale of the 1002nd Night
Right and Left and *The Legend of the Holy Drinker*
Job: The Story of a Simple Man
The Emperor's Tomb
Confession of a Murderer
The Radetzky March
Flight Without End
The Silent Prophet
Hotel Savoy
Tarabas
Weights and Measures
Zipper and His Father
The Spider's Web

What I Saw

Reports from Berlin
1920–1933

JOSEPH ROTH
translated with an introduction by
Michael Hofmann

German selection by Michael Bienert

W. W. NORTON & COMPANY
NEW YORK   LONDON

Map of Berlin, page 2: Pharus-Plan Fahrtfinder-Ausgabe Berlin [map], 1915. Courtesy of the Map Division, The New York Public Library, Astor, Lenox, and Tilden Foundations

Copyright © 1996 by Verlag Kiepenheuer & Witsch Köln and
Verlag de Lange Amsterdam
English translation copyright © 2003 by W. W. Norton & Company, Inc.
Translator's Introduction copyright © 2003 by Michael Hofmann
Originally published in German as *Joseph Roth in Berlin: Ein Lesebuch für Spaziergänger*

All rights reserved
Printed in the United States of America

For information about permission to reproduce selections from this book, write to
Permissions, W. W. Norton & Company, Inc., 500 Fifth Avenue, New York, NY 10110

Manufacturing by The Maple-Vail Book Manufacturing Group
Book design by Chris Welch
Production manager: Andrew Marasia

W. W. Norton & Company, Inc., 500 Fifth Avenue, New York, N.Y. 10110
www.wwnorton.com

W. W. Norton & Company Ltd., Castle House, 75/76 Wells Street, London W1T 3QT

2 3 4 5 6 7 8 9 0

Contents

Part VII   Berlin's Pleasure Industry

Part VIII   An Apolitical Observer Goes to the Reichstag

Part IX. Look Back in Anger

Translator's Introduction

The name *"Weimar Republic"* has a whiff of fragility, of scandal, of doom about it. It denotes a tiny period of German history, the years from 1918 to 1933; an interval of tremulous republican government, between monarchy and dictatorship, between one catastrophic war and the approach of another; but most of all a period that was fast and febrile and fun, and—popularized by the somewhat superficial and touristic versions of Christopher Isherwood—became practically synonymous with the Jazz Age or the Roaring Twenties. Historically, though, it was a form of government and a constitution. There is some pathos and idealism in the name "Weimar," the little statelet of Goethe and Schiller. One has to imagine the United States or Britain defeated in war, having taken enormous casualties, under part-occupation, and saddled with reparations in a punitive peace treaty that assigned them the guilt for the war, then, bethinking themselves of their finer traditions, naming their government and new constitution after a town that seemed to offer some literary precedent, as it might be "Walden" or "Stratford-on-Avon." In the end the literary and idealistic connotations of the name did nothing. The government was established (and occasionally maintained) by force of arms. The diplomat Count Kessler wrote witheringly: "The paradox of a republican-social-democratic government allowing itself and the capitalists' safes to be defended by hired unemployed and royalist officers, is simply too insane." But so it went, and the Weimar period as a whole was characterized by political violence, assassinations, inflation, unemployment, crisis, and instability. There were seventeen governments in fewer than fifteen years, as an anguished center fought off numerical and decibel encroachments from both flanks. Weimar was always unloved, always friendless. To quote the historian Peter Gay: "The Republic was born in defeat, lived in turmoil, and died in disaster."

BERLIN WAS BOTH a pendant and a totem for Weimar. It was the seat of government, and the place that made the government nervous like no other. It was where the Communist martyrs Rosa Luxemburg and Karl Liebknecht were murdered in 1919, and the Jewish foreign minister Walther Rathenau (see "A Visit to the Rathenau Museum") in 1922; and yet it was never a Brown—a Nazi—town. It may have celebrated its five hundredth anniversary some time in the 1980s, but it was only really around the turn of 1900 that its combined agglomeration and expansion began to exert the pull—in federated Germany, with its clutch of older, sometimes more beautiful cities—of a center. "To go to Berlin," writes Gay, "was the aspiration of the composer, the journalist, the actor; with its superb orchestras, its hundred and twenty newspapers, its forty theaters, Berlin was the place for the ambitious, the energetic, the talented. Wherever they started, it was in Berlin that they became, and Berlin that made them, famous." And yet there was something ungainly and sprawling and fermenting about it. It was a capital city that, like some horrible adolescent, had yet to grow into its role. In some ways it was even worse—a sort of golem—something that had been created for the purpose of existing, like Weimar, a bubble, and a hyperventilating bubble at that. (Read Roth on the Kurfürstendamm, an arrow going nowhere, but not a place one can *be*.) It is a very curious thing that the extraterritoriality that (West) Berlin had later, as an island-city in the Cold War, seemed already to exist in the 1920s, as witness the following tirade against Berlin, by the hero of Joseph Roth's 1927 novel, *Flight Without End:*

"This city," he said, "exists outside Germany, outside Europe. It is its own capital. It does not draw its supplies from the land. It obtains nothing from the earth on which it is built. It converts this earth into asphalt, bricks and walls. It shades the plain with its houses, it supplies the plain with bread from its factories, it determines the plain's dialect, its national mores, its national costume. It is the very embodiment of a city. . . . It has its own animal kingdom in the Zoological Gardens and the Aquarium, the Aviary and the Monkey House, its own vegetation in the Botanic Garden, its own stretches of sand on which foundations are laid and factories erected, it even has its own harbor, its river is a sea, it is a continent. . . . It nourishes the natives of Düsseldorf, of Cologne, of Breslau, and draws nourishment from them. It has no culture of its own as have Breslau, Cologne, Frankfurt, Königsberg. It has no religion. It has the most hideous churches in the world. It has no society. But it has everything that society alone provides in every other city: theaters, art, a stock-exchange, trade, cinema, subways."

THIS BOOK—THE first collection of Joseph Roth's journalism to appear in English—is a direct translation of a German selection made in 1996 by Michael Bienert: *Joseph Roth in Berlin*, subtitled *Ein Lesebuch für Spaziergänger* (a reader for walkers). It is, I think, an admirable selection, not least because Bienert is fully qualified to serve two masters: He has literary training, and he works, or has worked, as a tour guide in Berlin. He knows the city like the back of his hand. That said, the interests of the English-speaking reader, as I seek to represent them, are not fully identical with Bienert's. That reader is unlikely to turn up in Berlin with the *Lesebuch* in his or her hand, hoping to follow in Roth's footsteps and scope out his haunts; the *practical* dimension of the selection lapses in translation. It is still literary but no longer a guide, and I have not included Bienert's notes or introduction. (Perhaps I can further comfort American and English readers by observing that in most of these materials, he observes how irrecoverable and built over Roth's Berlin is: not surprising, given that even something as recent and physical as the Berlin Wall seems to have left no trace of itself after just twelve years.) Still, the selection stands. It is varied and purposive, stops long enough on occasion to allow Roth to contradict himself—though hardly ever to repeat himself—and covers the breadth of his perspectives admirably. It even seems to pick out a sort of narrative line in terms of mood and subject, widening and darkening from airily whimsical beginnings to take in exile, assassination, the spread of fascism, and the uncertain prospects for German-Jewish civilization.

JOSEPH ROTH WAS a newspaperman all his life. Of the two dozen or so photographs that exist of him, a surprising number show him holding a newspaper or reading one. He was a lifelong reader, writer, thinker, and apologist for the press, of almost whatever stripe. "But these newspapers find only vendors," he writes of enemy—nationalist—newspapers in "Election Campaign in Berlin." "I am their only buyer." In a sardonic note from his early days as a journalist in Berlin, he described himself as probably the only staffer who went out on the street after his shift, to hawk the paper! When he was a star writer for the *Frankfurter Zeitung*, earning one deutsche mark per line (he never sold himself short!), he still thought of himself as an "orchestra member." It was—not coincidentally—one of the great periods of German journalism. Even a selection like the present one, which can hardly have intended anything of the kind, seems to be full of references to newspapers—often aesthetic ones, on the effects of certain type designs and sizes. The note of anguish at the unceasing round of editions in Berlin in the "Kurfürstendamm" piece sounds utterly real to me; Roth had an advanced newspaper dependency, in several senses. In his life, he wrote hundreds and hundreds of articles for dozens of different papers. It was necessity and survival, but it was also more. No one who didn't believe in the trade as a vocation could have been so consumed by it, or would have written as he did in 1926, in his peppery letter style, to his *Frankfurter* editor, Benno Reifenberg:

> It's not possible to write feuilletons with your left hand, and one shouldn't *allow oneself* to write them on the side. That's a serious slight to the whole *form*. The feuilleton is as important as politics are to the newspaper, and to the reader it's *vastly more important*. The modern newspaper is formed by everything but politics. The modern newspaper needs reporters more than it needs editorial writers. I'm not a garnish, not a dessert, I'm the main course. . . . What people pick up the newspaper for is *me*. Not the parliamentary report. Not the lead article. Not the foreign news. And yet, in the editorial

offices, they go around thinking of Roth as a sort of eccentric chatterbox that they can just about afford as they're such a great newspaper. They are so mistaken. I don't write "witty columns." I paint the portrait of the age. That's what great newspapers are there for. I'm not a reporter, I'm a journalist; I'm not an editorial writer, I'm a poet.

Roth was a maximalist of the short form. Even at the very end, in exile in Paris, he was still contributing to émigré newspapers, in which he was read by colleagues and by a few handfuls of like-minded readers. It is a partial, and an interested, but to my mind a perfectly respectable opinion (held to by some readers and critics at the time) that Roth's masterpieces were not his novels but his feuilletons, in much the same way, say, that the American poet Randall Jarrell was said, by Helen Vendler and others, to have used his talent in his poems and his genius in his book reviews.

How he began is a little more mysterious. It is possible that he worked for the army newspaper in his time with the Austrian military, from 1916 to 1918. When he returned from the war in 1919, aged twenty-five, with nothing to his name but an unfinished degree, a few published poems and short stories, and his army experience—whatever it was—he settled into journalism as if to the manner born. His undated short story "Rare and ever rarer in this world of empirical facts . . .," with its ironic account of a demobilized and disoriented officer falling effortlessly into a rather inadequate career in journalism, may be a jocular reflection of what happened to Roth himself. Another, this time more swaggering, account is in his rightly celebrated letter to his publisher, Gustav Kiepenheuer, on the occasion of the latter's fiftieth birthday, on June 10, 1930, in which Roth remarks: "[Till I reached] Vienna, where, because I was broke, I started writing for the papers. They published my nonsense. It made me a living. I became a writer." In 1919 Roth wrote a hundred pieces for the newly founded Viennese paper *Der Neue Tag*. When it folded in April 1920, he moved to Berlin—home at the time to a dozen daily newspapers, and with a calmer rate of inflation than Austria's—and his production continued practically uninterrupted, for the *Neue Berliner Zeitung—12-Uhr-Blatt*, the *Berliner Tageblatt*, the *Berliner Börsen-Courier*, and others. And when in January 1923, newly married, he was signed up by the *Frankfurter Zeitung*, and with his first novel on the way, Roth had reached the peak of personal and professional contentment.

IT IS A SIMPLIFICATION, but not much of one, to say that Roth hated Berlin but permitted it to exercise him. Its inorganic history, its manic growth spurts, its indifferent aesthetics, its centralized pomp, its sporadic veneer of modernity, its human coldness, its callous officialdom—"Berlin is freezing," he said, "even when it's sixty degrees"—all variously appalled him, coming from Vienna and before that from Galicia. It is not surprising that the perspectives he seeks out are those of the unfortunates, the people who fall between the cracks, the immigrants, the Jews, the released lifer (a perspective taken up again in his novel *Rebellion*), the homeless living, and the nameless dead. And, conversely, that those that appall him are those of organized Berlin, as a center of fun, of transport, of government, of nightlife and literary life, and of sports. His natural sympathies were always with the outcast and the underdog, and Berlin gave him plenty.

Berlin is the metropolis as villain. It was always a sort of Moloch—Potsdamer Platz was the busiest square in Europe in

1914—and, then as now, a kind of ungovernable building site. A sort of moral ugliness and chaos seem to set it apart even from other negatively portrayed cities of the time as Paris (in Rilke's *The Notebooks of Malte Laurids Brigge*, and later dubbed "manic depressive capital of the world" by Henry Miller), as New York (in Henry Roth's *Call it Sleep*), as London (in Conrad's *The Secret Agent*), and as Oslo (in Hamsun's *Hunger*). "Who in all the world goes to Berlin voluntarily?" Roth asks in *The Wandering Jews*. Berlin is where people are forced to come, and then—like Geza Fürst in "Refugees from the East"—unhappily get stuck. The genetic code of its sprawl is simply abhorrent. This is not the conventional view of Berlin, which sees its size and roughness and celebrates them. That view is the one expressed by Hans Flesch von Brünningen, which was posted on the wall of an exhibition around Ernst Ludwig Kirchner's painting of Potsdamer Platz: gleeful awe, a presentiment of thrills, delirious hyperbole, a quivering response to an electromagnet of sin and careerism:

> The year was 1913. You have to realize what Berlin meant to us back then in Vienna. It was everything to us, really. For us, Berlin was crazy, debauched, metropolitan, anonymous, gargantuan, futuristic. It was literary and political and artistic (*the* city for painters). In short: an infernal cesspool and paradise in one. Together with a friend of mine I climbed the Glorietta Hill behind Vienna. It was nighttime. To the north, the sky was aglow. "That's Berlin," I said. That was where we would have to go.

Roth, one might surmise, felt somewhat similar in 1920 when he arrived, prepared, if need be, to live on cherries and sleep on park benches. Berlin, then, was where he was based until 1925, when he moved to Paris, although he remained a frequent visitor until the Nazis took power in 1933. However, only once (and only for a few months) did he and his wife have anywhere to call home; the rest of the time they stayed in hotels or with friends. This was admittedly a lifelong propensity of Roth's, but in the case of Berlin it perhaps lends a little further chill and exposure to his views. Anyway, the city became the altar on which his spontaneous humanity, his left-leaning politics, and his belief in progress were sacrificed.

THIS STORY OF disillusion and antipathy might promise to make for dreary reading, but in fact one's experience of these pieces is utterly unlike that. Not only is writing (and writing for immediate publication even more) a terrific discipline—Roth said the only way he understood the world at all was when he was holding a pen in his hand and had to write about it—more, the particular form, the feuilleton, in the hands of a master like Roth, seems to be a counterform. Inversion, reversal, subversiveness seem to be built into it. What is small is inevitably made to seem vast, and vast things are shrunk into a witty perspective. (Such subjects as the waxworks and the small-scale model of Solomon's temple are obviously quintessential Roth; but no less, perhaps, is the very large department store.) "Saying true things on half a page" was his working definition of the feuilleton, nothing more restrictive than that. It seems, in Randall Jarrell's tremendous phrase, "professionally surprising," so much observation, mobility, and unexpectedness inheres in it.

One proceeds by indirection: not Palestine but Grenadier-strasse; not the celebration of Berlin nightlife but a melancholy, serious, and Marxist analysis of mass-produced "fun"; not the successful and much-touted American film comedy but the

potency of the cheap music playing beforehand; not nostalgia but
the Gleisdreieck; nowhere celebrated but the little oasis called
the Schiller Park, "a park in exile"; the six-day races, yes, but also
the chauffeurs freezing outside. In this form Roth identifies
and liberates unexpected qualities in Berlin and the Weimar
Republic: the sadness of Ebert's death and the unexpected
decency of the mourning public; the excessive glory of technical
accomplishments; the sternly unglamorous tawdriness of crooks
and whores. Partly it is his position—he seems prepared to go
anywhere, talk to anyone, write about anything, in the most
exhilarating way—partly it is the unpredictability of the direction
he will take. This, the East German poet Heinz Czechowski
reminded me in his own fine selection of Roth's occasional writing, called *Orte* (places), comes down to "interest," *Interesse* in
German, *inter* plus *esse*, being between, in the midst, in the thick
of things. And that, too, is the best word for Roth, and for Roth
in Berlin—curving around past people's front rooms on the
S-Bahn, talking to a czarist colonel, composing a memorial for
Red Richard.

Michael Hofmann
London, December 2001

Part I

What I Saw

Going for a Walk

(1921)

W hat I see, what I see. What I see is the day in all its absurdity and triviality. A horse, harnessed to a cab, staring with lowered head into its nose bag, not knowing that horses originally came into the world without cabs; a small boy playing with marbles on the sidewalk. He watches the purposeful bustle of the grownups all around him, and, himself full of the delights of idleness has no inkling that he already represents the acme of creation, but instead yearns to be grown up; a policeman who fancies himself as the still point at the center of a whirlpool of activity, and the pillar of authority—enemy to the street, and placed there to supervise it and accept its tribute in the form of good order.

I see a girl, framed in an open window, who is a part of the wall and yearns to be freed from its embrace, which is all she knows of the world. A man, pressed into the shadows of a public square, collecting bits of paper and cigarette butts. An advertising kiosk placed at the head of a street, like its epigram, with a little weathervane on it to proclaim which way the wind is blowing down that particular street. A fat man in a cream-colored jacket, smoking a cigar, he looks like a grease spot in human form on this

summer's day. A café terrace planted with colorful ladies, waiting
to be plucked. White-jacketed waiters, navy blue porters, newspaper sellers, a hotel, an elevator boy, a Negro.

What I see is the old man with the tin trumpet on the
Kurfürstendamm. He is a beggar whose plight draws all the more
attention to itself for being inaudible. Sometimes the falsetto of
the little tin trumpet is stronger and more powerful than the
entire Kurfürstendamm. And the motion of a waiter on the café
terrace, swishing at a fly, has more content in it than the lives of
all the customers on the café terrace. The fly gets away, and the
waiter is disappointed. Why so much hostility to a fly, O waiter?
A war cripple who finds a nail file. Someone, a lady, has lost the
nail file in the place where he happens to sit down. Of course
the beggar starts filing his nails—what else is he to do? The
coincidence that has left the nail file in his possession and the
trifling movement of filing his nails are enough to lift him
about a thousand social classes, symbolically speaking. A dog
running after a ball, then stopping in front of it, static now and
inanimate—unable to grasp how some stupid, brainless rubber
thing only a moment ago could have been so lively and spir-
ited—is the hero of a momentary drama. It's only the minutiae
of life that are important.

Strolling around on a May morning, what do I care about the
vast issues of world history as expressed in newspaper editorials?
Or even the fate of some individual, a potential tragic hero,
someone who has lost his wife or come into an inheritance or
cheated on his wife or in one way or another makes some lofty
appeal to us? Confronted with the truly microscopic, all loftiness
is hopeless, completely meaningless. The diminutive of the parts
is more impressive than the monumentality of the whole. I no

longer have any use for the sweeping gestures of heroes on the global stage. I'm going for a walk.

Seeing an advertising kiosk on which facts such as, for instance, Manoli cigarettes are blazoned out as if they were an ultimatum or a *memento mori*, I completely lose my patience. An ultimatum is just as inconsequential as a cigarette, because it's expressed in exactly the same way. Whatever is heralded or touted can only be of little weight or consequence. And it seems to me there is nothing these days that is not heralded. Therein lies its greatness. Typography, to us, has become perspective, value. The most important, the less important, and the unimportant only *appear* to be important, less important, unimportant. It's their image that tells us their worth, not their being. The event of the week is whatever—in print, in gesture, in sweeping arm movements—has been declared the event of the week. Nothing is, everything claims to be. But in the face of the sunshine that spreads ruthlessly over walls, streets, railway tracks, beams in at the window, beams out of windows in myriad reflections, anything puffed up and inessential can have no being. In the end (led astray as I am by print, by the presence of typography as an adjudicator of value) I come to believe that everything we take seriously—the ultimatum, the Manoli cigarettes—is unimportant.

Meanwhile, at the edge of the city, where I have been told nature is to be found, it isn't nature at all, but a sort of picture-book nature. It seems to me too much has been printed about nature for it to remain what it used to be. On the outskirts of our cities, in place of nature, we are presented with a sort of idea of nature. A woman standing at the edge of the woods, shielding her eyes with the umbrella she has brought along just in case, scanning the horizon, and seeing a spot that seems familiar from some painting, exclaims: "Isn't this just so picturesque!" It's the degradation of nature to a painters' model. It's not such a rare degradation either, because our relationship to nature has become warped. You see, nature has acquired a purpose where we are concerned. Its task is to amuse us. It no longer exists for its own sake. It exists to satisfy a function. In summer it provides woods where we can picnic and doze, lakes where we can row, meadows where we can bask, sunsets to send us into raptures, mountains for walking tours, and beauty spots as destinations for our excursions and day-trips. We have Baedeker-ized nature.

But what I see hasn't made it into the Baedeker. What I see is the sudden, unexpected, and wholly meaningless rising and falling of a swarm of mosquitoes over a tree trunk. The silhouette of a man laden with firewood on a forest path. The eager profile of a spray of jasmine tumbling over a wall. The vibration of a child's voice, fading away into the air. The inaudible, sleeping melody of a distant, even an unreal life.

I don't understand the people I see putting their best foot forward to enjoy nature. There's a difference between a forest and a sidewalk. "Recreation" is no necessity, if that's the expressed objective of the hiker. "Nature" is no institution.

Western Europeans set out into nature as if to a costume party. They have a sort of loden-jacket relationship with nature. I saw hikers who were accountants in civilian life. What did they need their walking sticks for? The ground is so flat and smooth that a fountain pen would have served them just as well. But the man doesn't see the flat and smooth ground. He sees "nature." If he were going sailing, presumably he would don the white linen suit he inherited from his grandfather, who was also a weekend sailor. He has no ears for the plashing of a wave, and he doesn't know that the bursting of a bubble is a significant thing. The day that nature became a site for recreation was the end.

In consequence of which, my outing was that of a curmudgeonly soul, and I wish I hadn't undertaken it.

Berliner Börsen-Courier, May 24, 1921

Part II

The Jewish Quarter

2

The Orient on Hirtenstrasse
(1921)

I t's a grotesque contradiction, a spring evening in this part of
town whose grime and greasepaint don't so much conceal its
Levantine-working-class nature as emphasize it. Barely a hundred paces from Alexanderplatz and the U-Bahn and the S-Bahn,
it seems strange that the street names are still bland and
European. But if you take a right, you find yourself suddenly
immersed in a strange and mournful ghetto world, where carts
trundle past and an automobile is a rarity.

Polish Jewish children play in the middle of the road. From
time to time they set up a wailing or squawking. The old people
go their ways, completely unmoved by howling, children's games,
hoops, bobbing balloons. The old folks have more important
things on their minds: They are here on business.

Several traveling brokerages have been established here. For
example, there's one on the corner of Hirtenstrasse, which is
noteworthy because it's even more downbeat than the others,
giving it an oddly idyllic aspect. In all the other greater and lesser
exchanges in the small, narrow, grimy restaurants, there is a coming and going, an ebb and flow of human bodies, almost as in a
real exchange. But on the corner of the main street, there is the

tranquillity of a modest business. You can't pick anything up from the others, that's how intense and bewildering is the crush of people, words, prices. But at least where I am you can listen and look.

The owner of these premises is a Russian-Polish Jew with a velvet cap and a beard. He is sitting on a green corduroy sofa under a picture of Moses Montefiore, reading a newspaper. His spectacles are in pretty bad shape; their steel frames have a black thread bandage. He shows no interest in his clients, barely even bothering to reply to a greeting, and then only absent-mindedly, to do the other a favor, catching a greeting like a stray ball and tossing it back. The other doesn't bother to pick it up. He is in a hurry, he has seen an important personage. A personage . . .

This personage—well, his real name is something different, but we'll call him Baruch. Baruch is dressed in a very European manner, high style winds itself around his belly in the form of a belt, such a belt as no Kurfürstendamm Baruch would be ashamed to be seen in.

Baruch is fat, clean shaven, with a black-rimmed pince-nez, and his job is that of a middleman.

In the space of barely ten minutes you see him sitting at half a dozen different tables. With pencil and notebook. I am sure he must have done twenty-five deals in those ten minutes. Oh, Baruch!

The people you see here are Eastern grotesques: a poor, shriveled-up old lady who sells shoelaces for a living—and dabbles in stocks on the side. She discusses Romanian bonds and the state of the leu* with Baruch, and it's quite grotesque to see how that arbiter of the life and death of marginal currencies takes this shoelace lady *seriously*. And avails himself of the opportunity to

* Leu, plural lei: Romanian unit of currency.

buy—*patented fly buttons.* He goes so far as to try and woo the favor and the confidence of this old bat. Oh, Baruch! . . .

It's suppertime, but no one eats here. They have good bread, fish in various sauces, and sausage from Cracow. But the woman behind the counter is unemployed. From time to time one of the businessmen will buy a *schnapps* from her. A strong, Russian *schnapps.* The drinker tosses his head back, as if it were a bowling ball loosely attached at the neck. Then the drinker's eyes glisten, he goes *Ah!* a couple of times, and he leaves without paying. The woman doesn't write it down either; there's no need; the customer will pay.

There is little sign of suspicion. People here know one another. No one gives a hoot about the occasional European visitor. So what if he's a snoop—who cares? We don't do any shady business here, you can't pin anything on us. We're not black marketeers. We just enjoy one another's company.

And in truth this type of dealer is completely different from the run of black market salesmen. Wonderfully thoughtful eyes, formidable old skulls, the physiognomies of scholars and philanthropists. These trades are done on the side. Who knows? Perhaps these people actually have *lives* in their time off.

From time to time, one of them might pray. Stand in a corner, muttering to himself, whispering. His lips tremble, his words are gabbled, the prayer is long, and he needs to be finished. No time, no time! No one bothers him, everyone steers clear of him; the aura of divine worship surrounds him, and all thought of percentages is far from him. No sooner has he finished his evening prayer than his expression is once more of this world. He reopens his eyes to the light of these premises, and to the floating percentages.

The door is open. It never occurred to anyone to close it. Till eleven and beyond. It's not till half past that things start to get quieter. People trickle out into the night, drift around outside for a while, like large buzzing night insects.

Outside, a couple of policemen are on patrol. Then the man gets up from his green corduroy sofa, stows his fragile spectacles in their case, and slowly walks over to the door to lock up.

His wife counts empty bottles behind the bar. The bottles plink like keys on a glass piano.

Neue Berliner Zeitung—12-Uhr-Blatt, May 4, 1921

3

Refugees from the East

(1920)

F ürst Geza* (because in Hungary they put the surname before
the first name, and some whim of fate likes to give beggars
lordly attributes)—or, if you prefer, Geza Fürst—worked as a clerk
in a Budapest grocery from the age of eleven. When he was sixteen
the Hungarian Soviet Republic took over, and the grocery store
was shut down. For his part, Geza joined the Red Army.

When the counterrevolutionary forces gained power in
Hungary, Geza Fürst and his parents fled to the part of Hungary
that was occupied by Romania. The Romanians expelled the Fürst
family. Fürst *père*, a Jewish master tailor, moved to Slovakia with
his wife and four daughters, scissors, ruler, thread, needle, and
young Geza. The sixteen-year-old, having served in the Red Army,
could not go back to Budapest. Instead he made his way to Berlin.

Not, please understand, to remain here. The commissioner in
charge of demobilization wouldn't allow him to in any case. Geza
Fürst, now barely seventeen, wants to go on to Hamburg. He
wants to take ship, be a cabin boy. Is he supposed to go back to

---

* In Hungarian order, and to a German ear, "Fürst Geza" means "Prince
Geza," an ironic appellation for a penniless refugee.

A Jewish hotel on the corner of Grenadierstrasse and Hirtenstrasse.

twisting paper bags in a grocery store, pulling herrings out of barrels of brine by their stiff tails, or spilling raisins across a counter? Or go and get himself recruited again? Geza Fürst is perfectly right to want to go on a ship. Sirens toot, white chimneys belch smoke, ships' bells ring, and the world is never ending. Geza Fürst will make a first-class sailor. He has broad shoulders but is still light on his feet, and with his gray eyes he can already see boundless horizons and blue infinity.

However, Geza Fürst hasn't been able to get to Hamburg yet because he doesn't have papers.

Geza Fürst sleeps in a boardinghouse on Grenadierstrasse, which is where I met him. I met others besides him. That boardinghouse is currently home to 120 Jewish refugees from the East. Many of the men arrived straight from Russian POW camps.

Their garments were a weird and wonderful hodgepodge of uniforms. In their eyes I saw millennial sorrow. There were women there too. They carried their children on their backs like bundles of dirty washing. Other children, who went scrabbling through a rickety world on crooked legs, gnawed on dry crusts.

They were refugees. We know them as "the peril from the East." Fear of pogroms has welded them together like a landslip of unhappiness and grime that, slowly gathering volume, has come rolling across Germany from the East. A few clumps of them have come to rest for the time being in the East End of Berlin. A small minority of them are young and healthy, like Geza Fürst, the born cabin boy. Mostly they are old and frail, if not broken.

They come from Ukraine, from Galicia, from Hungary. Back home they fell victim, in their hundreds of thousands, to pogroms. The survivors make their way to Berlin. From here they head west, to Holland and America, or south, to Palestine.

The boardinghouse smells of dirty laundry, sauerkraut, and masses of people. Bodies all huddled together lie on the floor like luggage on a railway platform. A few old Jews are smoking their pipes. Their pipes smell of scorched horn. Squealings and screechings of children in the corners. Sighs disappear down the cracks between the floorboards. The reddish sheen of an oil lamp battles its way through a veritable wall of smoke and sweat.

Geza Fürst can't stand it anymore. He thrusts his hands into his frayed jacket pockets, and—a tune on his lips—goes out on the street to get some air. Maybe tomorrow he'll get a place in the hostel on Wiesenstrasse that's been set up for homeless Eastern Jews. If only he had papers. Because they're very strict over on Wiesenstrasse; they won't just take anyone who turns up.

All in all some fifty thousand people have come to Germany

from the East since the war. I have to say, it can seem as if there were millions. The impression of so much wretchedness is double, treble, tenfold. That's how much there is. Among the fugitives there are more workers and artisans than traders. According to the employment statistics, there are 68.3 percent workers, 14.26 percent wage laborers, and only 11.13 percent self-employed traders.

There are no jobs for these people with German companies, even though the only way they pose any sort of threat is if they are *not* allowed to work. Then of course they *will* become black marketeers, smugglers, and even common criminals. The Association for Eastern Jews in Berlin does all it can to persuade the authorities and public opinion that by far the best solution would be to disperse this newly arrived immigrant workforce over the entire German labor market. But even the expulsion of these people seems too difficult for the authorities to manage. Instead of authorizing the immediate departure of all those applying for an exit visa, the authorities do their utmost to slow down and prolong the process. The refugees spend weeks upon weeks here, literally dying on the charity of their fellow men before they are allowed to make themselves scarce. To date, 1,239 people have successfully negotiated Berlin without first starving to death.

In Wiesenstrasse, in what was once a hostel for the city's homeless, a shelter for Jewish refugees from the East has now been set up. They are bathed, disinfected, deloused, fed, warmed, and put to bed. Then they are offered the chance to leave Germany. It is quite one of the most blessed preventative measures for dealing with the "Eastern peril."

The odd one among these people will have intelligence and initiative. He will go on to New York and make a million.

Maybe Geza Fürst will manage to get to Hamburg and become a cabin boy—Geza Fürst, who may now be found walking up and down Grenadierstrasse, hands in his pockets, ex–Red Guard, adventurer, and pirate *in spe*. Recently I heard him singing a Hungarian song that contained these words: "The wind and I, we're two of a kind; / no house or yard or body to shed a tear over us. . . ."

Neue Berliner Zeitung—12-Uhr-Blatt, October 20, 1920

4

Solomon's Temple in Berlin

(1920)

King Solomon, famous for his sayings and judgments and for his authorship of the Psalms, reigned at a time when history was still proceeding backward, namely from 1015 to 975 B.C. He loved high life and splendor, and was open handed both to God and to his own subjects. The latter he presented with tax edicts and tithes, and the former with devout prayers and a magnificent temple. The king turned to his neighbors for the gold, marble, and similar materials he needed for his building projects. He built his royal palace with the aid of King Hiram of Tyre, and that proved what an untenable idea anti-Semitism is. Because what happened was that Hiram—as cunning as if he had been Solomon—extended King Solomon unlimited credit, and King Solomon—as green and naive as if he had been Hiram—drew and drew on it until the anti-Semite Hiram showed his true Jewish nature, called in his loan. Thus he was able to gain a score of fertile territories in the north of the Jewish kingdom, for King Solomon was unable to pay his debts. Altogether King Solomon behaved like a reckless baron. He had baronial manners, and if the swastika supporters had come across him, they would have had to change their views.

Herr L. Schwarzbach,* who hails not from Ophir but from distant Drohobycz, has undertaken to rebuild the Temple of Solomon, "in miniature, of course," as he says in his advertisement, on a scale of 1 to 70. L. Schwarzbach has worked nine full years on his construction of the Temple of Solomon. I looked at the photograph of this man who has given nine years of his life to building the temple of a deceased king, without even the prospect of an architectural diploma at the end of it. It's the photograph of a bearded Polish Jew with velvet cap and side curls and large, dark, philosophical eyes, in which speculation stands no chance against mysticism. His picture hangs above the table on which the Temple of Solomon is exhibited. And the whole ensemble is to be found in a little Jewish restaurant on the corner of Hirtenstrasse.

Tickets to Solomon's temple may be purchased either in the restaurant itself, or, for the more cautious, in Sternkucker's bookstore on Grenadierstrasse. Another two marks will buy a brochure, and a further two marks will buy one in Hebrew. The literature is essential if you want to know the Temple of Solomon. Without it one would be helpless as a bridegroom.

Herr L. Schwarzbach's Temple of Solomon is made of hard-wearing cardboard, painted in red and white and gold, and has any number of pretty doors and windows and towers and oriels, and is altogether good, true craftsmanship.† Slender little pillarets thrust upward to a thin arch they have grown expressly to support. Idiosyncratic battlements teeter aloft like little jokes

---

* Not necessarily his real name. In *The Wandering Jews*, he appears as Herr Frohmann; that is also the version to which W. G. Sebald went for his account of the model temple, in the fourth part of his novel, *The Emigrants* (p. 176).

† The German word *Kleinkunst*, literally "small art," contains an untranslatable pun on this religious miniaturist.

of God, at the expense of this building in his praise. Green quartz windows continually prepare one for prayer, the coolness of service and confirmation. Narrow flights of stairs swarm up the heights in even and obtrusive diagonals. Little houses surprise one with their illogical presence, like boulders in the middle of a path, on the smooth parquet of a quadrilateral courtyard. Alert watchtowers squinny out at the world around this restaurant table. A well, no bigger than a waistcoat button, harbors miniature deeps of water, all on a scale of 1 to 70. The whole thing, a Lilliputian institute, converts pomp into cuteness. A sweetly affecting pathos.

You may see:
the foundations, at an elevation of three hundred cubits, and five hundred cubits square, under which flows the river Kidron;
the entrance to the flower garden, "from where the scent of flowers came up into the Holy of Holies";
the seventy-one golden chairs for the judges of the Sanhedrin;
the women's courtyard, a square space "measuring 135 by 135 cubits";
the chamber for the Nazarenes, where they took their pledge not to drink wine, and not to cut their hair;
the fifteen steps of the Levites, on which the fifteen psalms were sung, one psalm on every step;
the watchtower where the priests kept watch while the sacrificial fire burned;
the roof of pure gold over the Holy of Holies, studded with spikes a cubit long, to keep away bad-mannered birds;
and finally the altar, which measured 32 cubits square.

No one comes to Hirtenstrasse to see the Temple of Solomon. The people are godless and republican. In the next room of the restaurant, drying tench lie on sticky plates and stick their forked tails into the air. Sorry preserves fill a terrine with their mourning. A woman's dress flops emptily over the back of a chair.

In the bar a group of people chew over the day's news and the exchange rates.

They don't talk about King Solomon the Wise, who was, I suppose, an aesthete and an eccentric. I can just see him sneaking into the "women's courtyard, measuring 135 cubits in length and 135 cubits in breadth," and, if there was no one watching, creeping into the flower garden to pluck an Oscar Wilde–style green carnation and pop it in his buttonhole.

Then he would have gifted the Queen of Sheba a wonderful golden roof. And in return Hiram set the bailiffs on him and made him the poorer by twenty estates. Twenty whole estates! . . .

That's how beautiful she was, the Queen of Sheba.

Neue Berliner Zeitung—12-Uhr-Blatt, October 2, 1920

5

Wailing Wall

(1929)

In these days when Jews are being killed in Palestine, I chose to go to Grenadierstrasse—not to Jerusalem. I had the feeling it was better to be with the bereaved than the dead. I paid a condolence call on Grenadierstrasse. It was a hot day. All the doors were open, as were many windows. There was a reek of onions, fish, fat, and fruit, of infants, mead, wash, and sewers. The Jews were milling or walking around in Grenadierstrasse, showing a clear preference for the middle of the road over the sidewalk, and most of all for the edge of the pavement. They formed a kind of running commentary to the pavement. A kind of traffic fixture on Grenadierstrasse, cause unknown, and purpose mysterious; as if, for instance, they had been taken on by the Jewish faith to demonstrate some particular ritual. Women and children clustered in front of fruit and vegetable stands. Hebrew letters on shop signs, nameplates over doors, and in shop windows, put an end to the comely roundness of European Antiqua type with its stiff, frozen, jagged seriousness. Even though they were only doing commercial duty, they called to mind funeral inscriptions, worship, rituals, divine invocations. It was by means of these same signs that here offer herrings for sale, phonograph records,

The view along Grenadierstrasse from a window on Münzstrasse.

and collections of Jewish anecdotes, that Jehovah once showed himself on Mount Sinai. With the help of these terrible jagged letters he gave the Jews the first terrible moral law, for them to spread among the cheerful, blithe peoples of the world. It takes, I thought, a truly divine love to choose this people. There were so many others that were nice, malleable, and well trained: happy, balanced Greeks, adventurous Phoenicians, artful Egyptians, Assyrians with strange imaginations, northern tribes with beautiful, blond-haired, as it were, ethical primitiveness and refreshing forest smells. But none of the above! The weakest and far from loveliest of peoples was given the most dreadful curse and most dreadful blessing, the hardest law and the most difficult mission: to sow love on earth, and to reap hatred.

No! If Jews are being beaten up in Palestine, there is no need to go to Jerusalem and study the question of the British Mandate to understand why. It's not only in Jerusalem that there is a Wailing Wall. Grenadierstrasse is one Wailing Wall after another. The punishing hand of God is clearly visible over the bent backs of the people. Of all the thousand ways that they have gone, and go, and will go, not one is a way out, not one leads to a concrete, earthly goal. No "fatherland," no "Jewish homeland," no "place of refuge," no "place of liberty." There are various opportunities to discern the so-called will of history. And nowhere does it show itself as plainly as in all the many Grenadierstrassen in which Jews don't so much live as drift up and down. (Theirs is no pathological-degenerative unrest so much as a historically conditioned one.) Clearly it is the secret "will of history" for this people to have no country to live in but to wander the roads. And that daunting will corresponds to the daunting constitution of the Jews. In seeking a "homeland" of their own, they are rebelling against their deeper nature.

They are no nation, they are a kind of supranation, perhaps the anticipation of some future form of nation. The Jews have already lived through all the others: a state, wars, conquests, defeats. They have converted infidels with fire and sword, and many of them also have been converted to other religions, by fire and sword. They have lived through, and emerged from, their primitive periods of "national history" and "civic culture." The only thing that was left to them is to suffer as strangers among strange peoples, because they are "different." Their "nationalism" is of no material kind. There is not even an absolute physical identity in common; not even a fixed form of belief. The religion of their forefathers has softened into the common daily life of the descendants; it has become a way of life, of eating, of sleeping and sexual conjunction, of trading, or of working and studying. Only, the conditions of their external surroundings were more tempting and more binding than the laws that were left of their religion. It is impossible to adhere to these laws and live. And, above all the commandments of the Jewish faith, there is the supremely implacable commandment: to live. Every day demands a further concession. It's not that they fall away from the faith of their fathers—their faith falls away from them. Or: It becomes sublimated in their descendants. It determines the way they think, act, and behave. Religiosity becomes an organic function of the individual Jew. A Jew fulfills his "religious duties," even if he doesn't fulfill them. Merely by being, he is religious. He *is* a Jew. Any other people would be required to affirm their "faith" or their "nationality." The Jew's affirmation is involuntary, automatic. He is marked, to the tenth generation. Wherever a Jew stops, a Wailing Wall goes up. Wherever a Jew settles down, a pogrom goes up. . . .

It should be understood, at long last, that Zionism can only be a bitter experiment, a temporary, opportune degradation of Judaism, or perhaps merely the reversion to a primal, long since outmoded, form of national existence. Maybe it has succeeded in arresting or delaying the "assimilation" of Jewish individuals or groups. But in return it seeks to assimilate an entire people. If it appeals to the war-like traditions of Judaism, then one should counter that the conquest of Canaan is less of an achievement than the Bible, the Psalms, and the Song of Songs; also, that the present of the Jews is greater, possibly, than their past: being more tragic. . . .

It might even be more "practical" in a "political" sense, if the young Jews who are "going back" to Palestine today, did so as the grandchildren not of the Maccabees, but of the priests and prophets. In the course of my wanderings through the Jewish ghetto in Berlin, I bought some Jewish nationalist newspapers from Eastern Europe. Their reporting of the fighting in Palestine was indistinguishable from the war reports we read in our German newspapers. In the same dreadful Borgis bold type, in comparison to which spilled human blood seems a pretty thin and inconsequential fluid, those Jewish nationalist newspapers report on the Jewish "victories over the Arabs." And in the war correspondents' familiar gobbledygook you could read, in appalling black on white, that these were, thank God, not pogroms, but honest-to-goodness "battles." Here you could finally understand that the view of the Jews as cleverer than other peoples is erroneous. Not only are they not cleverer, they are even sometimes more stupid. They aren't ahead of the times, but if anything lagging behind. They are aping the recently failed European ideologies. Now, of all times, they are setting about their original Jewish steel baths. Of course it's only natural that they should put up a fight in Palestine. It's too bad that they were attacked. But to have their heroism confirmed to them in the newspapers—having been uncommonly heroic over thousands of years without journalistic clichés—that furnishes final proof that there are no seven wise men of Zion directing the destiny of the Jewish people. No, there are several hundred thousand idiots of Zion, who have failed to understand the destiny of their people.

Das Tagebuch, September 14, 1929

Part III

Displaced Persons

6

Nights in Dives

(1921)

The epicenter of the phenomenon known to us as the dive or joint is the Alexanderplatz station (exit Münzstrasse), from where it spreads over the east end of Berlin, and, from there, ultimately, over the rest of the world. It is also quite unthinkable without Neue Schönhauser Strasse, from whose cobblestones—as if they had been lampposts, or some other organic outgrowth of the street—arise pimps and their prostitutes, and the police station, whose gates are already locked and guarded by a couple of Berlin's finest. What these two policemen are dreaming of is a cigarette (they aren't allowed to smoke on duty) or an hour in a red-light bar, instead of a tart you can quickly feel up while her pimp is—unconscionably or conscientiously—detained in some gateway, tying up a cigarette deal. Nor can I imagine nights in dives without Weinmeisterstrasse, whose corners are always thick with bad characters. And certainly not without the police spy, in mufti but uniformed, incognito and unmistakable, the tips of his moustache giving away his loyal service and watchman's vigilance, authority and certainty in his expression, looking out for anyone with any hesitation about him. And even if he were less obtrusive, better camouflaged than he is, I would still know him by his footfall and his expression, by the fearlessness of his looming up suddenly from a bar or a back wall. The others don't have that fearlessness—they're just bold as brass.

Café Dalles

The premises of the Café Dalles at 13 Neue Schönhauser Strasse used to be called the Angels' Palace. Things change. For a time it was a public dining place, and I think that was probably its original function. Angels' palaces don't come purpose-built: Instead they come with long passages whose farther end, like a lake's opposite shore, is obscured by clouds of smoke, and with another entrance on the left, which may have been used as a *chambre séparée* for after-hours angels, and today has a roulette table and roulette games on the walls, folksy glass-fronted cabinets, with hand-painted picture postcard backdrops, harmless playthings to encourage an underage public.

Kirsch the burglar and Tegeler Willy and Apache Fritz are sitting at a table together, while the policeman stands and watches. At the bottom of the well-like passage, Elli's sitting on someone's lap, because she's got new stockings today. If you've got new stockings, you've got to show them off. Her little blond ringlets are combed down into her face. They hang there a little stiffly, like starched ruffles. I really think she wants nothing more from the world than to have half a kümmel inside her, and the knowledge that there is another half to come. Let her have it, please. My friend buys her some bread and butter. Now I think she's happy beyond dreams. New stockings, a kümmel, and some bread and butter. It really is an angels' palace.

Though I can't say what terms Kirsch is on with the police just now—there seems to be a standoff with the policeman at least—

Kirsch may be planning some new heist, or he's talking about some perfectly innocent game of cards, or maybe he's about to exit left, in the direction of the roulette table. To the right of the entrance, there's someone playing the piano, and Kirsch passes the hat around for him. Maybe he feels he has to be involved in some way. Everyone gives him something, either out of respect or because they want to contribute, even if they can hardly hear the music. Its thin sounds come swaddled in cigar smoke like cotton.

Reese's Restaurant

Reese's Restaurant is awash in red light. All the lamps have deep red paper napkins thrown over their shoulders like cloaks, and there's a band on stage, and the clientele is somewhat more refined. Reese's is an establishment you *visit.* The others are bars you *drop in.* When you go to Reese's, you first take a deep breath. And generally you go after 8 P.M. And the band is called "orchestra."

Also, you can take your hat off at Reese's without the risk of anyone staring. From time to time, descending from westerly spheres, a card sharp will put in an appearance. And it's not Kirsch who'll pass the hat around for the musicians, but a man armed with little green numbered boxes. That's how they do things at Reese's.

At Reese's the guests may be "politely requested to pay their reckoning promptly," but the waiter is well bred enough to take himself off if it doesn't happen that way. At Reese's you wear an outfit if you're a lady, and the waiter may even occasionally say, "The lady, please!" But the lady will address the waiter by his first name. New stockings are no rarity at Reese's.

Plus you can go up three steps to the back room, where they

play skat. That young reprobate actor who's quite talented is a regular here. He's getting together a foursome for skat.

Sometimes politics and crime mix at Reese's. I saw Kern again here. I'd last seen him in Vienna and Budapest. Those were revolutionary times; I found myself behind bars once in Hungary. . . . At Reese's the band plays without a break, and they are all in black. They don't have a bandleader, but the violinist keeps them in good order by looking at them. They play well.

From time to time there's even a little scandal at Reese's. Always a matter of honor. Never money, just women.

That's Reese's Restaurant for you.

Albert's Cellar

By contrast Albert's Cellar in Weinmeisterstrasse is quiet, no music, no red lights. The owner is a Romanian immigrant by the name of Albert. Albert's Cellar is an easy name to remember.

Albert's Cellar has regulars of such fixed habits that they even have their mail sent there. Certain aspects of Albert's Cellar are reminiscent of a writer's café. For instance, it is possible to sleep away an entire afternoon in Albert's Cellar. Paul was just embarking on his fourth hour when we arrived. He lay with his head slumped on the table, as though he were trying to saw through the fake marble with his nose. Beside him Regine, resplendent in her fake diamonds, was watching over his sleep. Paula was there with her pimp. He drank a glass of beer, slapped her on the back, and said: "Good luck then, girl." She sat in a dirty blouse, with spongy, droopy breasts, and drank up my friend's coffee. The day before yesterday she'd been at a fancy place on Hirtenstrasse where they had good coffee. She didn't like the coffee here at all, Yuck! Another girl was leaning against the iron stove. She was shivering quietly, and when she spoke (only to say, "How's it going?"), you saw that she didn't have any teeth. Her Rudolf had a mouth full of fillings—a treasure chest, not a mouth.

Therese is a peroxide blond, and I walk her over to her turf on Alexanderplatz. She's in a crisis just now. Rudolf's girl was locked up, and since he was on his own, he took on Therese. But then the original girl was let out (after just a week), and she had more experience and a better figure. So Rudolf was dumping Therese. She's looking for support. "He's got no character, Rudolf," she says. "He could have discussed it with me."

Yes, I quite agree, Rudolf's got no character. How can you be so unprincipled as always to put your business first?!

I cross my fingers for Therese so that she'll find someone. And then she'll be happy. I think she has character.

The Cigar Box

Even the world of dives has its symbols and its holy signs. A drum, for instance, is the emblem for a stout, respectable club with gold lace. And the sign of a burglar is a cigar box.

The cigar box contains not Dutch cigars but, arranged by size: "rippers" and "jacks" and "little aldermen." Or: "jimmies" and "claw-jimmies."

Because in the world of dives, even housebreakers' tools have their nicknames. A picklock is a little alderman, a crowbar is a jimmy, and a drilling tool—which admittedly has become almost obsolete as a tool of civilization—is a ripper. A man who works with rippers cannot gain my respect. He's a dinosaur. A self-respecting man earns his living with explosives, oxygen and dynamite. A ripper—get away!

The cigar box also contains a few S-hooks. S-hooks are so

called because they have the shape of a roman S. An S-hook is enough to take care of your average apartment door. Franz, though, never carries any S-hooks. He opens apartment doors that get in his way with his penknife. Franz is a skilled operator!

Franz always keeps his cigar box in his jacket pocket, but he's not one for symbols. He doesn't *need* any cigar box. After all, he's Franz! . . .

A cigar box—it needs to be old and battered, and to have a warped lid straining against the hinges—that's the trademark and the emblem. It can't be any old box!—not a cigarette box, for sure! It needs to be an honest-to-God *cigar* box.

You see: A man who crosses the threshold *without* a cigar box—what can he be? A pimp at best! The owner of the dive will say, "Well, how's business?" with a measure of condescension, as though patting the new arrival on the back with each syllable. Whereas a man who walks in with a cigar box will find the way opening up before him, and riffraff like pimps will give him a wide berth. That's the aura of the cigar box. You wouldn't believe what a humble cigar box is capable of. It's an emblem of authority, and for every uninitiated new arrival in the world of dives, it's like a case in which he carries his field marshal's staff. All honor to the cigar box!

On Mulackstrasse

Eleven at night, and Mulackstrasse looks like part of an archaeological site. A streetlight on the corner of Schönhauser Strasse squinnies across at it apprehensively. A girl patrols up and down, like a pendulum in her regular unceasing motion, as if she'd been set going by some invisible clockwork.

On the opposite corner is Willy's bodega. Hans, Willy's assistant, is there too. He has the most exquisitely parted and Bryl-creemed and innocently styled hair. And Gustav, the lithographer, feels utterly at home. He wears soft felt slippers, and his face is like a stubble field in autumn.

Willy is a bookie. Once, a couple of officers came his way, who shouldn't really have had any business dealing with bookies. Willy was just greeting a friend getting out of a car. The car impressed the officers. They concluded that a bookie who had a friend who owned a car couldn't really be a bookie. They left Willy some money. An awful lot of money. And then Willy scrammed.

"Long Hermann" rolls up at about half past eleven. He has a very placid, broad face. His eyes are tiny and unfocused; it's as though they were hiding behind a soft veil of tears, to see without being seen.

And just then Gustav disappears. I don't know what Gustav gets up to in the cellar.

The Tippel Pub

The Tippelkneipe, or Tippel Pub (on Linienstrasse), is where panhandlers and street sweepers go to drink. Panhandlers wear baggy clothes, with plenty of room in them for "stray merchandise." They're all thin and frozen; they feel the cold in every pore. The heat of ten African summers wouldn't be enough to thaw them out. It can't be easy, being a panhandler.

They play cards. On the table the grimy bits of cardboard make a noise like muffled slaps.

Fred and Karlchen are not panhandlers. It's nice of them to be sitting here at all. By the grace of God, they don't need to be here. Fred and Karlchen: They must make a couple of hundred marks a day.

Fred and Karlchen work in the west. As lightbulb specialists. Only expensive houses.

The passages in these expensive houses often have electric light. Karlchen will hop up on Fred's shoulder and unscrew the bulbs. There are a couple of businesses on Elsasser Strasse that will pay *four to six marks apiece* for bulbs. The electricians don't ask where the bulbs come from. Electricians are not curious people by nature.

Now do you see that it's nice of Fred and Karlchen to spend their time here? Playing skat with panhandlers?

It's very quiet in the Tippel Pub. An old dog is stretched out in front of the iron stove. The smack of the cards doesn't bother him in the least. It's a dog's life for me! he thinks.

Gipsdiele

So called because it's on Gipsstrasse. If only everything in life were as straightforward!

I like it very much in the Gipsdiele. It's a cosy sort of place, small and tight, and the man behind the bar—who looks like a little costume-party beer barrel that somebody's stuck a head on—occupies a substantial portion of it himself. He doesn't leave much room for the other twenty or so people here.

I have a lot of old friends here. There's Big Max, the plasterer (his day job, anyway); Grete, whose real name is Margot; Little Bertha, Else (no surname); and finally Annie—Annie from Silesia, as opposed to Bavarian Annie.

It's important not to get those two mixed up. Bavarian Annie has her turf next to Schönhauser Tor, and is never seen around here. Besides, she's only been back for a week. She claims she was banged up in prison, but I don't believe her. I'm sure she was banged up another way, as Max says, and is back from the hospital but is embarrassed to say so.

Annie from Silesia is counting her money. When I look across at her, she stops. I don't know why—I'm not going to tell anyone.

Someone's set down his cigar box and orders a couple of kümmels. The order and the setting down of the box have made a big hole in the general conversation: There's silence for a moment. A man wearing a hotel porter's visored cap is racking his brain: Now, what was he in for?

Max says to the man in the cap: "I need a woman and a claw-jimmy." The claw-jimmy won't be a problem. As early as tomorrow. But a woman—apparently that's not so easy.

In case of any misunderstanding, Erna screeches: "I'm spoken for!" Erna loves Franz. Erna got a gold filling a week ago, and she hasn't stopped laughing since. She can't just let her mouth hang open like a hungry crocodile's! Oh, no! So if the world is to see her gold filling, Erna will just have to laugh. Erna laughs at the saddest things.

Franz is big and wide and has just walked in. For a moment or two, he completely fills the little bar with his personality. He radiates authority. All the pimps shrivel up and dwindle away like rubber balloons.

Erna gets a poke in the ribs that sends her sprawling along the bench. But Erna laughs. . . .

Neue Berliner Zeitung—12-Uhr-Blatt, February 23/28, 1921

7

With the Homeless

(1920)

The Declaration

Case No. . . . P. B.

Was heard by the court in Berlin, on . . . 1920.

Mr. [No Name] was instructed to find himself alternative accommo-
dation within five days, failing which, notwithstanding the most
strenuous efforts on his behalf to do so, he would be punished for mak-
ing himself homeless. The appellant was further warned that in
accordance with #361, subsection 8, of the Criminal Law of the
German Empire, such punishment will consist of up to six weeks in
prison, and, in accordance with #362 ibid., transferral to the police
authorities, for placement in a workhouse.
approved and signed.
Signature of the homeless man in question.
Signature of the police case worker.

Here is to be found the true cause of the Homeless Revolt of
two days ago in Fröbelstrasse. The rioters were for the most part
young people, egged on by a somewhat colorful individual from
East Prussia. The young homeless held a meeting in Weissensee,
and decided to storm the shelter. An official who tried to placate

them was so badly beaten that he ended up in hospital. The police were called. A few of the miscreants have already been taken into custody. It is unlikely that they will all be caught.

The document quoted above is the so-called declaration, which has to be signed by anyone entering the homeless shelter on Fröbelstrasse. The German in which this philanthropical document is couched corresponds to the philanthropy it expresses. The youthful quasi revolutionaries certainly did not rise up because they were critical of its grotesque style or the solecisms of its humanitarian mission. They just wanted to let off steam—to prove they were people "to be reckoned with," and, broadly, to remind themselves (and others) of the existence of the republic. But the physical expression of their indignation would be understandable (if not condoned), if it were just that, honest indignation and not a result of the unscrupulous conduct of an unethical individual. "Failing which"—and if someone were unable to prove that despite all his endeavors he had not found himself an abode—is six weeks in prison really appropriate punishment for that? Is punishment appropriate at all? Isn't it rather the case that *finding* accommodation within five days in Berlin these days should be taken as proof of criminality? This is an old and musty decree, and it is finally on its way out. Now, after a conscientious and humane official has found himself the victim of violence unleashed in those whom the law has left with no other option.

The Building

Red brick. The chill uniform of stern durability in which our state institutions, hospitals, prisons, schools, post offices, and churches show their character. A garden's autumnal colors are a vain effort to lend a pleasant or stirring aspect to what remains, all too evidently, a state enterprise. The building remains brick red, and looks as though it's been plonked down in the middle of nature. Fröbelstrasse, by the way, is in a part of Berlin where that brick-red atmosphere tends to dominate. On the right a board fence rings a bit of—hardly—open ground, and further on, a caravan, evidently the property of tinkers. Prenzlauer Allee owes its alluring name to the presence of a few scrawny trees, sprung from the stones of a city precinct, trees not by nature but by municipal decree. Then the hospital at the front, the shelter for the homeless at the back. At the entrance the police have a pleasant greeting for all those merely going by. The corridors are bare, their faces pancaked over with official white. The chief inspector, a large, kind, fair-haired man, is full of understanding because he has seen so much already. All the officials wear humanity under their uniforms. Anyone called upon to supervise misery will view criminality differently. All state officials should be required to spend a month serving in a homeless shelter to learn love.

The Dormitory and the People in It

The dormitory is vastly long and relatively narrow. You could easily take a walk in it, if it weren't for the two rows of beds jutting out, barracks-style, from either side. A line of beds runs down the middle too. Naked iron bedsteads, wire-mesh beds for penance. Every homeless person is given a thin blanket of papery stuff, which, admittedly, is clean and disinfected. And on these beds they sit and sleep and lie, the homeless people. Grotesque-looking figures, as though hauled from the lower depths of world literature. People you wouldn't believe. Old graybeards in rags, tramps hauling a motley collection of the past bundled up on their crooked backs. Their boots are powdered with the dust of decades. Middle-aged men, with sunburned faces chiseled by hunger and toughness. Young fellows in baggy pants, with eyes that look at you with a mixture of fear and confrontation. Women in brown rags, shameless and shy, curious and apathetic, quivering and resigned. A hundred of them to a room. Women, grown men, and youths kept apart. It takes about two hours to fill an intake. Admission is between four in the afternoon and nine at night. Everyone is given a steaming bowl of soup. Anyone who looks particularly wretched, a little more. Every morning there's a sick call. There are always plenty of applicants. Many are footsore. Some of these people have walked all their lives. Roughly half have sexually transmitted diseases. The majority have lice. It's difficult to persuade them to get cleaned up. Their clothes don't survive disinfection. They'd rather go around with their lice intact than look still more ragged than they do already.

The Families

Families are accommodated in separate wooden cubicles that are set up in the halls. A few look almost cosy. Every corner of the hall has a gas burner and a little range at which the women can do their cooking. Washing is hung up to dry in the miasma of cooking smells, digestion, and communal living. Every little room has a gaslight. The people here are refugees. From Prussia, from the Rhineland, from Holstein. They know one another. They pay calls on one another. Some may have brought along a few sticks of furniture they've salvaged from somewhere, others have managed to acquire this or that. I can picture the women arguing among themselves, over a child or a cooking pot, say. Poor people come to blows over such little things. The children are fair-haired and slightly dirty. They don't have any nice toys. Their world consists of a courtyard, a dozen bits of gravel, a tree, and one another. The one another is the best of it.

The Lieutenant Colonel

I sat with him, in his little wooden cubicle. Lieutenant Colonel Bersin is a czarist Russian officer, and a refugee. He has been in Berlin since April. He is old and stiff and proud. His gait is a little crooked, but after all the world has become so crooked. Revolution! Little Father is no more. Where is the czar? Where are his epaulettes? Where is the General Staff? He is a veteran of the Chinese war, the Japanese war, the Great war. He was lieutenant colonel on the General Staff. Most recently in Riga. He speaks excellent German but is still pleased that he can speak to me in Russian. He has newspapers and books piled up next to his bed. He reads everything he can lay his hands on. His officer's cap is on the wall. He shows it to me with a great deal of pride, touching pride, like a child showing off his drum. He would like to work. He wishes he didn't have to be a burden on the city. He is a lieutenant colonel. How much longer can the Bolsheviks last? Only a little bit, surely! It's insane! A revolution! Ripping the epaulettes off officers' uniforms! Where is the czar? Little Father? Where is Russia? He has a family. His children—perhaps they are married by now; or fled, or even dead! What sort of world is this? A crooked world! Poor, poor lieutenant colonel! History has performed a somersault, and a lieutenant colonel winds up in the shelter for homeless people.

Thousands of people used to pass through the homeless shelter. Now there are a thousand every night. In the morning two or three of the dormitories are combed by the police. They find the people they have been looking for, sometimes.

Others they don't bother with at all. They know who they are. They have been coming to the shelter for ten years now, or more. Residents. Resident homeless. The provisional or the contingent has become their normal way of life, and they are at home—in their homelessness.

Neue Berliner Zeitung—12-Uhr-Blatt, September 23, 1920

8

The Steam Baths at Night

(1920)

The steam baths in the Admiral's Palace are once more open all night. During the war their nighttime hours were first curtailed, then stopped altogether. Now you can *take a steam bath at night.*

Before the war a visit here represented the inevitable and indispensable conclusion to a night on the town, and the rejuvenation or rehumanizing of the night owl. Yesterday is swilled off him into the basins, and he emerges from the waters of the Admiral's Palace clean shaven, reconsecrated, ready for fresh deeds, into the morning air of Friedrichstrasse. The steam baths consituted the break—the "clean break"—between the bacchanals of the night and the day's gainful employment. It interposed itself between the bar and the desk. Without its ministrations—cast your minds back—it would have been impossible to sustain a rowdy nightlife with anything like the same stamina.

Nowadays, with the domestication of pleasure, with the fact that contemporary man no longer needs to bathe in pure waters, the steam baths have been turned into a night shelter. If you can't find a hotel room, you go to the baths. One night costs twenty marks. For that you can sweat the night away, if you like, or sleep

The men's lounge in the Admiral Baths.

yourself clean. The baths should have some sort of inscription. Something like: PER SUDOREM AD SOLEM! or WHITE NIGHTS.

Travelers may be seen arriving from the nearby Friedrichstrasse station at midnight, with suitcases. Returned from fruitlessly making the rounds of the city's hotels, they sigh with relief at the entrance to the baths. Slowly they have become a pivotal metropolitan institution—a bolt- and water hole for the tourist in his hour of need.

The grotesque spectacle of a hot room at night, containing sixteen naked homeless people, trying to sweat out the soot and coal smoke of a train journey, gives rise to a positively infernal range of interpretations. A series of illustrations, say, to Dante's journeys in the underworld. The only creature permitted to be fully clothed, standing there purposefully and conscientiously with scrubbing brush and torturer's gauntlet in hand, could quite easily be some underdevil, if you happened not to know that his infernal character will be appeased, and his true character revealed by a small tip, once you have withstood his torments.

I don't know if people in hell look as ridiculous as they do here. If the fashion there is for them to be likewise stripped naked, then they will do, for all their grimness and tragedy. I have a feeling that the witching hour does something to exacerbate the already intrinsically comical condition of nudity. It's such a bizarre notion that between midnight and 2 A.M. there are people being steamed.

Somebody with frail, uncoordinated joints that look as though they'd been provisionally held together with string performs swimming motions in a pool for a whole nocturnal hour. Another, a fat man, who might be advised to borrow the equator from the earth as a belt for his dressing gown, looks on with a grimly sadistic expression, until he starts to feel the chill and has to take himself to the hot pool to recoup the calories that his Schadenfreude has cost him. He cautiously extends the tip of his right big toe into the water, but it's too hot for him. He would like to watch himself enter the water—only his belly isn't made of glass.

The dormitory looks like a hollow polygon from geometry class. The sofas are small, low, and numerous. They stand there, as it were, guilelessly, as if, say, somebody had just left them there in despair, because there was nowhere else. People come here in their Turkish towels to try and catch a little sleep.

Only they make it impossible for one another. It is quite extraordinary what hidden desires cleanliness is able to flush out of thoroughly sweated souls. The appetite increases prodigiously. I almost think the only reason the steam baths were closed during the war was because of England's naval blockade. Sixteen thoroughly purified men are capable of consuming at a single sitting enough food to feed a city for six months.

Oh, and if only sandwiches didn't have to come wrapped in noisy wax paper! As if soft, silent paper wouldn't do the job just as well! Three gentlemen who have gotten off the train ask for their bags. I hoped one of them would have the provisions for all three in his bag. I hoped, further, that hunger would appear in all three *simultaneously*, since they'd all arrived on the same train, and stepped out of their baths at the same time too. But they, cunning fellows, used their appetites to provoke and taunt me.

Each of the three took it in turn to open his suitcase, his little key squeaking in the lock like a young puppy dog, and then came the unwrapping, with all the lavishly variegated stages of a proper picnic lunch, as if this weren't a steam bath at night but a green meadow on a Sunday afternoon.

Over time I grew able amply—hardly—to distinguish the three travelers from one another. One of them unwrapped his sandwiches swiftly and with decision, he didn't rustle so much as crunch. The other didn't crunch, but he was impatient and kept ripping his paper. The third took the longest. He folded up his paper minutely afterward. I think he must have had a long journey still ahead of him. Strange, someone taking so much trouble to make it clear to all those present that he didn't really need to take a bath here. No, by no means. He was clean only yesterday. Who would doubt it? But an odd, enforced bath like this, for want of a hotel room, it's not such a bad thing. And even though I'm absolutely prepared to believe that he was in a state of tiptop cleanliness when he arrived, he still won't stop trying to convince me of the fact. He comes from the provinces. It all strikes him as terribly amusing, and I can see

him working on his account for the assembled listeners in the bar—
the wacky things people get up to in Berlin.

You can sleep quite well on these sofas, if your neighbors have
already eaten. If you go out in the corridor, you will see a poster
that tells you that it is forbidden, first, to smoke (where would
you keep your cigarettes?), and second to enter the manicure
room "in a state of undress." And for all that I saw naked people
leaving the manicure room.

People in a state of nature wander through the corridors of the
Admiral's Palace. The world's highways and byways must have
looked like this when the world was in its infancy, and before men's
and women's fashion became the flourishing industry it is today.

If you go out onto the dark streets at 5 A.M., you will just catch
the final farewells between men and women, and the tired home-
ward trudge of a Friedrichstrasse whore who's had a bad night
and is going home penniless. A truck rumbles past, it's raining,
and it's bitter.

Neue Berliner Zeitung—12-Uhr-Blatt, March 4, 1920

BERLIN, Schillerpark, Momentaufnahme von der Planschwiese.

9

Schiller Park

(1923)

Schiller Park opens its portals, quite unexpectedly, in the north of the city, a surprising gem beyond the brewery belt of the various Schultheisses and Patzenhofers: like a park in exile. It looks every bit as though it had once been situated in the west of the city, and along with its banishment, it had been stripped of its ornamental lake and its little weather hut with barometer and sundial.

What it's left with are its weeping willows and its complement of park wardens. These are laconic and, in all probability, good people, because they follow an occupation that is not a soul-destroying one. They are the world's only harmless police, admonitory notice boards put in place by the Almighty and the local authorities, till one day, out of boredom, they suddenly left their posts and took to ambulating up and down the leafy avenues. On their faces you can read their original, now weathered inscription: CITIZENS, LOOK AFTER YOUR AMENITIES—and the willow wands they hold in their hands are mildly waving exclamation marks. Park wardens, by the way, are the only living beings permitted to set foot on the grass.

I have long been curious as to what park wardens do in the winter. It's scarcely credible that they should ever leave their parks to share a kitchen with wives and children. Much more likely that they wrap themselves in straw and rags, and passersby take them for rose trees or bits of statuary, or that they dig in for the winter, and come out in the spring along with the violets and primulas. With my own eyes I have seen them feeding off hips and haws, in the manner of shy forest creatures. Ask them a question, and they will think for a long time before replying. There's always a layer of solitude about them, as there is with gravediggers and lighthouse keepers. . . .

The people who live around Schiller Park work in the mornings. That's why the park is as deserted at that time as if it were off limits. One or two unemployed men trudge past; otherwise I see no one.

Then two girls, seventeen and nature-loving, come wandering through its avenues. It's as if birches could suddenly walk. But real birches are rooted in the ground, and can only sway their hips.

The children arrive at three in the afternoon with pails and shovels and mothers. They leave the mothers sitting on wide white benches and toddle off to the sandbox.

Sand is something that God invented specially for small children, so that in their wise innocence of what it is to play, they may have a sense of the purposes and objectives of earthly activity. They shovel the sand into a tin pail, then carry it to a different place, and pour it out. And then some other children come along and reverse the process, taking the sand back whence it came.

And that's all life is.

The weeping willows, on the other hand, are evocative of death.

They are a little contrived, a little exaggerated, still green in the middle of all the colors of autumn, and there is a human pathos to them. Weeping willows were not created by God at the same time as the other trees, like the hazelnuts and the apple trees, but only after he had decided to allow people to die. They are a sort of second-generation tree, flora endowed with intellect and a sense of ceremony.

Even in Schiller Park the leaves drop from the trees in a timely fashion, in the autumn, but they are not left to lie. In the Tiergarten, for instance, a melancholy walker can positively wade through foliage. This sets up a highly poetic rustling and fills the spirit with mournfulness and a sense of transience. But in Schiller Park, the locals from the working-class district of Wedding gather up the leaves every evening, and dry them, and use them for winter fuel.

Rustling is strictly a luxury, as if poetry without central heating were unnatural.

The rosehips look like fat red little liqueur bottles, distributed for promotional purposes. They fall from the trees free of charge, and are collected by the children. The park wardens look on, feeling no alarm. For they have placed their trust in the Lord, who feeds the wardens in the fields and arrays them in local-authority caps.

Berliner Börsen-Courier, October 23, 1923

10

The Unnamed Dead

(1923)

The city's unnamed dead may be seen laid out, in tidy rows, in the photograph cabinets on the ground floor of the police headquarters. It's a grisly exhibition drawn from the whole grisly city, in whose asphalt streets, gray-shaded parks, and blue canals death lurks with revolver, chloroform, and gag. This is the hidden side of the city, its anonymous misery. These are her obscure children, whose lives are put together from shiftlessness, pub, and obscurity, and whose end is violent and bloody, a murderous finale. They stumble unconsciously into one of the numberless graves that have been dug beside the path of their lives, and the only trace of themselves they bequeath to posterity is their photograph, snapped at the so-called scene of the incident by a police photographer.

Each time I stop in front of a photographer's window to view the pictures of the living in their finery, the newlywed couples, the confirmees, the smiling faces, the white veils, the confetti, the rows of medals on some excellency's breast, the sight of which seems to tinkle and jingle in the mind's ear—I remember the case with the dead in the police station. It shouldn't be in the corridor of the police station at all, but somewhere where it is very visible,

79

in some public space, at the heart of the city whose true reflection it offers. The windows with the portraits of the living, the happy, the festive, give a false sense of life—which is not one round of weddings, of beautiful women with exposed shoulders, of confirmations. Sudden deaths, murders, heart attacks, drownings are celebrated in this world.

It is these instructive photographs that should be shown in the Pathé Newsreels, and not the continual parades, the Ascension Day celebrations of patriotism, the health spas with their drinking fountains, their parasols, their bitter curative waters, their terraces from Wagner myths. Life isn't as serenely beautiful as the Pathé News would have you believe.

Every day, every hour, a great many people, many hundreds of people, pass through the corridor of the police headquarters, and *no one* stops in front of the glass cases to look at the dead. People go to the Alien Registration Office,* to the Passport Office to get a visa, to the Lost Property Office to look for an umbrella, to the Criminal Investigations Department to report a robbery. The people who come to police headquarters are concerned, in one way or another, with life, and with the single exception of your correspondent, not one of them is a philosopher. Who among them would take an interest in the dead?

These dead people are ugly and reproachful. They line up like prickings of conscience. They look as they did when they were first found, mortal terror on their faces. They stand there open mouthed, their dying screams are still in the air, you can hear them as you look. Their death agonies keep their eyes half open, the white shimmers under their eyelids. They are bearded and

---

* Including Joseph Roth himself: As an Austrian journalist, he was required to pay regular calls on Prussia's finest.

beardless, men and women, young and old. They were found on the street, in the Tiergarten, in the river Spree or the canals. In some cases the place where they were found is not given or is unknown. The drowned bodies are puffed up and slime encrusted, they resemble badly mummified Egyptian kings. The crusts on their faces are cracked and split like a poor-quality plaster cast. The women's breasts are grotesquely swollen, their features contorted, their hair like a pile of sweepings on their swollen heads.

If these dead had names, they would be less reproachful. To judge by their faces and garments, they were not exactly prosperous in life. They belonged to those called the "lower classes," because they happened to be worse off. They were laborers, maids, people who have to undertake heavy physical labor or crime if they are to live. It is unusual for one of the dead heads to emerge from a stiff collar, which in Europe is the emblem of the middle class. Almost always from open-collared shirts in dark colors that show the dirt less.

And the place where their gruesome death caught up with them, that now seems to color their entire lives. One was found on December 2, 1921, in the Potsdam Station toilets. On June 25, 1920, this woman, age unknown, was pulled ashore on the *Reichstagsufer* of the Spree. On January 25, 1918, that bearded, toothless head died on Alexanderplatz. On May 8, 1922, this young man with a rapt expression died, on a bench on Arminiusplatz. He must owe his peaceful countenance to that wonderful May night on Arminiusplatz. Probably a nightingale was singing when he died, the lilac was fragrant, and the stars were shining.

On October 26, 1921, a man, aged about thirty-five, was beaten to death on a piece of waste ground, somewhere off Spandauer Strasse. A thin line of blood leads from the temple to the lip, thin and red. The man himself has long since been buried, and his blood has stopped, but here in the picture it will always flow. Futile to wait for cranes, like the legendary cranes that once revealed the identity of the murderer of Ibycus. No cranes swarm over the waste ground off Spandauer Strasse—they would long ago have been roasted and eaten. God, beyond the clouds, watches the conflagration of a world war quite unmoved. Why would he choose to get involved over one poor individual?

There are perhaps one hundred photographs in the display cases, and they are continually being replaced by others. Thousands of unknown people die in the city. Without parents, without friends, they lived lonely lives, and no one cared when they died. They were never part of the weave of a society or community—a city has room for many, many lonely people. If a hundred of them are murdered, thousands live on, without a name, without a roof, like pebbles on the beach, practically indistinguishable one from another, all one day to meet a violent end— and their death has no particular resonance and never makes the newspapers like that of some Talat Pasha.

Just one anonymous photograph making its mute appeal to indifferent passersby in the police station, vainly asking to be identified.

Neue Berliner Zeitung—12-Uhr-Blatt, January 17, 1923

Part IV

Traffic

IM STRUDEL

DES VERKEHRS

REGIE: LEO PEUKERT

UFA-LEIH

Verleihbetrieb der Universum-Film Aktiengesellschaft

11

The Resurrection

(1923)

A Half Century in Prison

The Berlin old people's home is situated on the main street in Rummelsburg, where the first glimmering green of the world beyond factories just begins to show. As the name suggests, old people live there. They have set down their pasts like heavy burdens that they have successfully dragged to their final destinations. There's not far to go now, from the old people's home to the grave.

A good many of these old people are actually going back into care. They were institutionalized as juvenile delinquents, then were released out into the world, were picked up and sent back to where they had started. On fine evenings the oldsters sit on benches in the big park, and tell each other about different worlds, about Mexico, or Spain, or the various Capes of Good Hope that they made for in their lives, on whose rocks they beached. The old people's home is destiny. A man can have wandered many thousands of miles in his life, but in the end he will wind up in Rummelsburg. It lies at the end of every adventurous life. You can't escape the Rummelsburg your destiny holds for you.

There is one man living in the old people's home in Rummelsburg, who can look back on a fifty-year death. What for others is the end, to him is the beginning. This old people's home is, so to speak, his kindergarten. At the end of fifty years this man of seventy is facing a new world.

The man's name is Georg B., and he was sentenced to life imprisonment fifty-one years ago for being an accessory to robbery and murder. Recently the authorities were in a good mood, and he was released and allowed to go to Rummelsburg. And, at the end of fifty-one years, he found himself back, for the first time, in the great city of Berlin.

This account of a resurrection is only possible because the extraordinary rarity of such a "case," while not compensating for the man's past as a violent criminal, at any rate pushes it into the background. He has been sufficiently punished for his crime, and the interesting part of his story would not have been possible without crime and without punishment.

Georg B. remembers Berlin the way it was fifty years ago. If, in the course of his long life behind bars, he thought of the city at all, then he saw before him a city with horse-drawn traffic in its streets, a city that ended at Potsdamer Platz, and the clatter of a cart would have struck him as a metropolitan noise indeed. For fifty years B. carried the picture of such a city in his head. If at times he ventured to imagine progress, if he happened to read in the pages of some newspaper that had been picked up and dropped in his remote fastness, about technical innovations, then his imagination might conjure up maybe a four- instead of a three-story house, and his eye might envision, perhaps, without the incremental aid of reality, a vehicle that was capable of moving by itself. A vehicle whose speed would correspond, perhaps, with that of a carriage drawn by four, or at the most, six, horses.

For what else did his understanding have to guide him than the scale of what he knew? A dray horse represented speed to him— and he had never seen a human move more nimbly than a hare, a deer, a gazelle.

Then, all at once, B. climbed out of the S-bahn, and stood in the middle of the twentieth century. Was it the twentieth? Not the fortieth? It had to be at least the fortieth. With the speed of arrows shot from a bow, like human projectiles, young fellows with newspapers darted here and there on flying bicycles made of shiny steel! Black and brown, imposing and tiny little vehicles slipped noiselessly down the street. A man sat in the middle and turned a wheel, as if he were the captain of a ship. And sounds— threatening, deep and shrill, plaintive and warning, squeaking, angry, hoarse, hate-filled sounds—emanated from the throats of these vehicles. *What were they shouting?* What were these voices? What were they telling the pedestrians? Everyone seemed to understand, everyone except B. The world had a completely new language, a means of communication as universal as German— and yet it was composed of anguished, shattering primal sounds, as from the first days of mankind, from the deceased jungles of the Tertiary period. One man stopped, and another sprinted, arms across his chest, cradling his life, right across the Damm. Potsdamer Platz was no longer the end, but *Mitte*.* A wailing hoot from a policeman's cornet gave the orders for quick march and attention, a whole assembly of trams, cars crushing one another's rib cages, a flickering of colors, a noisy, parping, surging color, red and yellow and violet yells.

And then a network of wires overhead, a slashed and cross-hatched sky, as though some engineer had scrawled his

* A play on words: "middle" and the name of a Berlin district.

deranged circuits across the ether. If you pressed your ear against a pole, you could hear strange noises within, ghostly voices, as if whole African tribes were howling in blood lust or worship, and you could hear them here in Berlin.

Georg B. bought himself a subway ticket and stood in bewilderment on the platform, allowed himself to be pushed onto a train, and then he thought the underworld had gone crazy too. Could the dead still sleep undisturbed? Were their bones not being rattled in their graves? Did the roar of a train not infect their silence? And what kept the upper world from collapse? How could the road fail to shatter every time a train passed below, throwing thousands of people, cars, horses, wires, and everything else to perdition?

Georg B., the seventy-year-old, wanders around like a youngster. He wants to work. Energy bottled up inside him for half a century seeks to express itself. Who would believe him? In his bewilderment he's not allowed to stop and draw breath. Is he dying? Is he facing his own end? The experience of this century mocks human laws. Experience was stronger than death. The conquest of the city is followed by the conquest of work. Man, surrounded by machines, is compelled to become a machine himself. His galvanized seventy years are fidgeting, banging, shaking. B. must work.

Neue Berliner Zeitung—12-Uhr-Blatt, February 24, 1923

12

The Ride Past the Houses

(1922)

The S-Bahn line goes right past the houses, affording its passengers many curious and interesting sights—especially in springtime, when walls are prone to indiscretion, when casements reveal the idylls behind, and courtyards betray their secrets.

Sometimes a ride on the S-Bahn is more instructive than a voyage to distant lands. Experienced travelers will confirm that it is sufficient to see a single lilac shrub in a dusty city courtyard to understand the deep sadness of all the hidden lilac trees anywhere in the world.

Which is why I return from a ride on the S-Bahn full of many sad and beautiful impressions, and when I navigate a little bit of the city, I feel as proud as if I had circumnavigated the globe. If I imagine the courtyards a little more gloomy, their lilac trees a little scrawnier, and the walls a couple of yards higher and the children a shade or two paler—then it's as though I'd been to New York, having sampled the bitterness of the metropolis, because most major discoveries can be made very locally, either at home or a few streets away. Phenomena and atmospheres and experiences differ not in their essence, but in secondary qualities like scale.

Electric S-Bahn train and steam train together.

A wall has a physiognomy and a character of its own, even if it doesn't contain a window or anything else that reinforces its connection to life, beyond a billboard for, say, a brand of chocolate, placed so that its sudden flash on our retina (yellow and blue) will make an indelible impression on our memory.

Behind the wall, meanwhile, people will be getting on with their lives, little girls will be doing their homework, a grandmother will be knitting, a dog gnawing its bone. The pulse of life will beat through the cracks and pores of the silent wall, break through the tin simulacrum of the Sarotti chocolate, beat against the windows of the train, so that their clatter acquires a vital, human sound and makes us hearken at the proximity of a related life so close at hand.

It's a curious thing, how much the people who live in houses bordering the S-Bahn resemble one another. It's as though there were a single extended family of them, living along the S-Bahn lines and overlooking the viaducts.

I have come to know one or two apartments near certain stations really quite well. It's as if I'd often been to visit there, and I have a feeling I know how the people who live there talk and move. They all have a certain amount of noise in their souls from the constant din of passing trains, and they're quite incurious, because they've gotten used to the fact that every minute countless other lives will glide by them, leaving no trace.

There is always an invisible, impenetrable strangeness between them and the world alongside. They are no longer even aware of the fact that their days and their doings, their nights and their dreams, are all filled with noise. The sounds seem to have come to rest on the bottom of their consciousness, and without them no impression, no experience the people might have, feels complete.

There is one particular balcony with iron bars, like a cage hung in front of the house, and in one particular place on it, all through the spring and summer, hangs a red cushion, rain or shine, like an implacable fleck of oil paint. There is a courtyard that is quite crisscrossed with clotheslines, as if some monstrous antediluvian spider had spun its stout web there from wall to wall. A dark blue pinafore with big white dobs of eyes always billows in the breeze there.

Over the course of my rides, I've also come to know a little blond girl. She sits by an open window, pouring sand from little toy dishes into a red clay flowerpot. She must have filled five hundred of those flowerpots by now. I know an old gentleman who spends all his time reading. The old man must have read his way through all the libraries of the world by now. A boy listens to a big phonograph on the table before him, its great funnel shimmering. I catch a brassy scrap of tune and take it with me on my journey. Torn away from the body of the melody, it plays on in my ear, a meaningless fragment of a fragment, absurdly, peremptorily identified in my memory with the sight of the boy listening.

There are only a few who have nothing to do, and just sit at their windows and watch the trains go by. That tells you how boring life would be without work. Therefore every one of us has a purpose, and even animals have their use. There is no lilac tree in a backyard that doesn't support drying laundry. That's the sadness of those backyards: How rare it is for a tree to do nothing but bloom, to have no function but to wait for rain and sunshine, to receive them both and enjoy them, and put forth blue and white blossoms.

Berliner Börsen-Courier, April 23, 1922

13

Passengers with Heavy Loads

(1923)

Passengers with heavy loads take their place in the very last cars of our endless trains, alongside "Passengers with Dogs" and "War Invalids." The last car is the one that rattles around the most; its doors close badly, and its windows are not sealed, and are sometimes broken and stuffed with brown paper.

It's not chance but destiny that makes a person into a passenger with heavy baggage. War invalids were made by exploding shells, whose destructive effect was not calculation but such infinite randomness that it was bound to be destructive. To take a dog with us or not is an expression of personal freedom. But being a passenger with heavy baggage is a full-time occupation. Even without a load, he would still be a passenger with heavy baggage. He belongs to a particular type of human being—and the sign on the car window is less a piece of railway terminology than a philosophical definition.

Baggage cars are filled with a kind of dense atmosphere you could cut maybe with a saw, a freak of nature, a kind of gas in a state of aggregation. The smell is of cold pipe tobacco, damp wood, the cadavers of leaves, and the humus of autumn forests. What causes the smell are the bundles of wood belonging to the

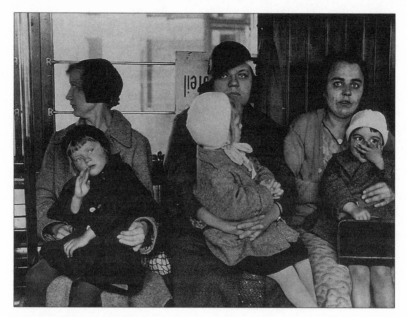

Travelers on the S-Bahn.

occupants, who have come straight from the forests, having escaped the shotguns of enthusiastic huntsmen, with the damp chill of the earth in their bones and on their boot soles. They are encrusted with green moss, as if they were pieces of old masonry. Their hands are cracked, their old fingers gouty and deformed, resembling peculiar gnarled roots. A few leaves have caught in the thin hair of an old woman—a funeral wreath of the cheapest kind. Swallows could make nests for themselves in the tangled beards of the old men. . . .

Passengers with heavy loads don't set down their forests when they themselves sit down. Having to pick up one's load again after a half hour in which one's spine has felt free for all eternity seems to weigh heavier than an entire pine forest. I know that with us soldiers, when a few minutes' rest beckoned after hours of marching, we didn't undo our packs but continued to drag them with us like a horribly loyal misfortune,* or a foe to whom we were bound in an eternal alliance. That's how these old bundle carriers sit, not so much passengers with heavy loads, as heavy loads with passengers. And that also goes to demonstrate the fatefulness of carrying loads, that it's a condition rather than an activity. And what do the forest people talk about? They speak in half sentences and stunted sounds. They keep silent not from wisdom but from poverty. They reply hesitantly, because their brains work slowly, forming thoughts only gradually, and then burying them in silent depths no sooner than they are born. In the forests where their work is, there is a vast silence unbroken by idle chatter; there the only sound is that of a woodpecker attacking a branch. In the forests they have learned that words are useless, and only good for fools to waste their time on.

But in the scraps these people do say is expressed the sorrow of an entire world. They have only to say "butter," and right away you understand that butter is something very remote and inaccessible, not something you spread with a knife on a piece of bread, but a gift from heaven, where the good things of this world pile up as inaccessibly as in a shop window. They say: "Summer's early this year"—and that means that they'll be going out into the forests looking for snowdrops, that the children will be allowed out of bed to play in the street, and that their stoves can be left unheated till the autumn.

Actors, who relate their woes in many clever sentences and

---

* From time to time, Roth comes quite close to Rilke. Cf. lines 16–17 of the first of the *Duino Elegies: "und das verzogene Treusein einer Gewohnheit, / der es bei uns gefiel, und so blieb sie und ging nicht."*

with much waving of hands and rolling of eyes—they should be made to ride in the cars for passengers with heavy loads, to learn that a slightly bent hand can hold in it the misery of all time, and that the quiver of an eyelid can be more moving than a whole evening full of crocodile tears. Perhaps they shouldn't be trained in drama schools but sent to work in the forests, to understand that their work is not speech but silence, not expression but *tacit* expression.

Evening comes, an overhead light goes on. Its illumination is oily and greasy; it burns in a haze like a star in a sea of fog. We ride past lit-up advertisements, past a world without burdens, commercial hymns to laundry soap, cigars, shoe polish, and bootlaces suddenly shine forth against the darkened sky. It's the time of day when the world goes to the theater, to experience human destinies on expensive stages, and riding in this train are the most sublime tragedies and tragic farces, the passengers with heavy loads.

Of all the labels and bits of jargon, the verbose or laconic edicts that regulate the bustle of a city, providing information and instructions, offering advice, and constituting law—of all the impersonal formulations in stations, waiting rooms, and the centers of life—this one is humane, artistic, epigrammatic, concealing and revealing its huge content.

The honest man who came up with "Passengers with Heavy Loads" for practical purposes can't have known that at the same time he found a title for a great drama.

This is how poetry is made.

Berliner Börsen-Courier, March 4, 1923

14

Some Reflections on Traffic
(1924)

For the past several months, the question of traffic control has been painfully acute in Berlin. Important stretches of major roads are blocked off to traffic of all kinds. Potsdamer Platz looks like a suppurating wound.* And day after day, night after night, workmen scrabble around. It is now two weeks since the traffic control tower was put up. One had an expectation, perhaps, of something soaring and magnificent. But one day there stood a little gray metal stump of a tower, with large, and at that stage, still-closed round eyes on its top edge. Those eyes, sending out colored beams, were meant to regulate the traffic automatically. But instead the traffic regulator remains the blond, chunky policeman on his wooden platform. In the newspapers there are reports almost every other day of street-car collisions. (With the compensation sums that are paid out every year to the victims of accidents in Berlin, one could set up a traffic system truly worthy of a great city.) Experts were paid to go out into the world to make studies of traffic systems

---

* When last seen, (August 2001), it still did.

Roadwork in 1930.

in great cities. When they got home, they produced a new traffic plan in which a proliferation of confused paragraphs collided
like so many streetcars. A few newspapers set up squeals in
"Cicero bold"—as if it were they themselves that had been run

over. With mighty capitals* from the arsenal of typesetting, they crushed the new traffic plan. They ran responses from hackney-coach drivers, chauffeurs, bus drivers, and motorists; and if the traffic plan hadn't been withdrawn, then they would have summoned fresh evidence from people who weren't affected by them either: chimney sweeps, presumably, exterminators, hairdressers—why not?—and others would have been solicited for their unprofessional opinions. . . . It was a chance to prove all over again that they were not going to let up on those in power. It could have been a chance to offer more advice and less of a tongue-lashing. But good advice is as expensive as bad mockery is cheap. . . .

I'm not offering my thoughts on traffic in Berlin with the clear conscience of an expert, convinced he has something helpful to say, but with the right of the lay person, who is a victim of the bad traffic and who even faces the prospect of eventually becoming something of an expert in it (given his protracted education in poor conditions and various experiments). By the time the streetcars of this city finally become completely unnegotiable, I'll probably be able to drive one myself. Today I only know what I see and suffer. And that's sufficient authority.

It seems to me that the use of streetcars is incompatible with the traffic levels of a metropolis. In an age of air travel they are the equivalent of post coaches. Generally the tracks they run on go down the middle of the street. If there happens to be another vehicle on the tracks, they're stuck behind it. They block the pedestrian's view so that he won't see a vehicle coming toward him on the other side of the street. They stand motionless, as

---

* Two more of those typographical references that appear so often in Roth's journalism.

though rigid with fear, for minutes on end, making a wall with little cracks in it through which it would be possible to force one's way, only one is wary of being swiped by a rapidly approaching car from the other side. This defect of the streetcars is so blatant that even the experts seem to be aware of it. Therefore they are thinking of abandoning the streetcars for omnibuses. But it's a very long way from having an idea to putting it into practice—a way, as it were, to be covered by streetcar. And in the meantime cars are proliferating, and on December 1 the tax on them is being cut, so that motor cabs will become (comparatively) afford-able, thereby adding a further complication to this already highly complicated situation.

Berlin has very few trained traffic policemen. There is no "traffic police" as such, only an administrative department that consists of a few specialist civil servants. Traffic duty is done by regular policemen, as it were, on secondment. And these good and eager fellows tend to wave their arms about with unneces-sary, vague flourishes. They aren't precise, and therefore produce confusion and misunderstanding. In the dark—a further source of trouble and grief—they are hard to make out. They are at con-stant risk of being run over themselves. Their gray-green uni-forms merge into the gray night. They are generally sharp, "bright," and independent-minded enough to use a little flexibil-ity in the way they interpret the regulations. But they are also called upon to supply information and to bring irate drivers to their senses. And all the time ill-considered newspaper articles undermine the authority of the police, and any heavy-goods driver you ask will invariably claim to be in the right as opposed to the policeman, who can see more of a scene because he is standing right in the middle of it. He ought to be more economi-cal with his movements and gestures. After dark a flashlight would be a useful thing, or, better yet, some proper street light-ing. Even some populous and quite central parts of Berlin still look like the deepest and darkest of provinces after nightfall. The economizing of the city authorities must have cost quite a lot of people their lives.

Worst of all are the slow roadworks. I know of no other city where the streets are patched as glacially slowly as they are in Berlin. There are some corners where the paving stones are care-fully lifted out every night and put back in the morning. Around midnight ten or twelve workmen start to lever out the paving stones and lay them by the side of the road. Then work begins on the underpinnings of the street, and on the streetcar tracks. Before the first tram comes through in the morning, the street has to be smooth again. It's like replacing bandages every day after an operation. And there are too few men. Sometimes you see a sorry little bunch—three or four fellows—standing on a corner lifting stones either with some rudimentary equipment or even with their bare hands, pouring tar, eerily and garishly lit by bright darting flames, looking like bizarre seekers after treasure, lonely, mysterious, and contemplative.

These are a few of the more visible defects, and their causes. But there are other factors besides, which materialists would laugh to scorn, there are—I should like to whisper this, if only one could write in a whisper—there are: *psst! metaphysical factors.*

Much of the trouble and irritation in daily public life is the fault of the public, in other words the undisciplined character of the postwar generation, the bitterness that erupts out of people. I will be so bold as to offer this theory: that a bus full of rancorous, quarrelsome, and aggressive passengers is bound sooner or later to have a collision. The mood of the passengers communicates itself to the driver. Everyone is fed up. No one offers his seat to a woman. Everyone is at odds with everyone else. People send one another furious looks. This one is taken for a Jew, that one for a "Bolshie." This lady's fur is provocatively expensive. The woman sitting next to her is not only furious—which one could understand—she makes no secret of her fury. A mildly intoxicated bowling team boards the bus. They announce their political views at the tops of their voices, because that's the most provocative way. If a woman is wearing a hat, they will stare her in the face. If she has a male escort, so much the better! At last a long-desired pretext for a quarrel or a fight. A catastrophe always seems just around the corner. You read the paper over the other man's shoulder. You press him into the corner or against the side of the bus. You are your neighbor's not keeper but policeman. If he stumbles, you shout at him to hold on to something. Everyone is an officious amateur conductor, and says: "Go to the back of the bus." But because the other man is also an amateur conductor, he won't do what you say.

Above all there's a lack of personal discipline, manners, decorum, natural discretion. If everyone causes their own individual catastrophes, how can there fail to be more general catastrophes? After all, the passengers on a bus or streetcar make up a community of a kind. But they don't see it that way, not even in a moment of danger. As they see it they are bound always to be the others' enemy: for political, social, all sorts of reasons. Where so much hate has been bottled up, it is vented on inanimate things, and provokes the celebrated perversity of inanimate things. Sending experts into other countries won't help much, so long as each individual refuses to work out his own personal traffic plan. There is a wisdom in the accident of language by which there is a single word, "traffic," for movement in the streets, and for people's dealings with one another.

On top of all the chronic traffic ailments of Berlin mentioned already, there is a new and acute one that threatens to eclipse them entirely. The subway is going on strike. The subway is Berlin's most important traffic artery. The streetcar companies and the management of the bus companies have put out all their available vehicles. But they are not enough. The crush is extraordinary even when the weather is cool and dry. If we should get a wet November day, then there will be the long awaited gridlock. The Ministry of Labor is supposed to arbitrate in the conflict, but the employees of the Berlin subway have let it be known that they will not be bound by its decision. This seems to have provoked a catastrophic torpor in both the Ministry of Labor and the management. There is no movement, even though a strike by the Berlin subway is not just a private matter between employers and employees, but one that affects the welfare of the city, and even of the whole country.

Frankfurter Zeitung, November 15, 1924

15

Affirmation of the Triangular Railway Junction
(1924)

I affirm the triangular railway junction. It is an emblem and a focus, a living organism and the fantastic product of a futuristic force.

It is a *center.* All the vital energies of its locus begin and end here, in the same way that the heart is both the point of departure and the destination of the blood as it flows through the body's veins and arteries. It's the heart of a world whose life is belt drive and clockwork, piston rhythm and siren scream. It is the heart of the world, which spins on its axis a thousand times faster than the alternation of day and night would have us believe; whose continuous and never-ending rotation looks like madness and is the product of mathematical calculation; whose dizzying velocity makes backward-looking sentimentalists fear the ruthless extermination of inner forces and healing balance but actually produces life-creating warmth and the benediction of movement. In the triangles—polygons, rather—of tracks, the great, shining iron rails flow into one another, draw electricity and take on energy for their long journeys and into the world beyond: triangular tangles of veins, polygons, polyhedrons, made from the tracks of life: *Affirm them with me!*

They are stronger than the weakling who despises them and is afraid of them. They will not merely outlast him: They will crush him. Whoever is not shattered and daunted and uplifted by the sight of them does not deserve the death that the divine machine is preparing for him. Landscape—what is a landscape? Meadow, forest, blade of grass, and leaf of tree. "Iron landscape" might be an apt description for these playgrounds of machines. Iron landscape, magnificent temple of technology open to the air, to which the mile-high factory chimneys make their sacrifice of living, broody, energizing smoke. Eternal worship of machines, in the wide arena of this landscape of iron and steel, whose end no human eye can see, in the horizon's steely grip.

Such is the realm of the new life, whose laws are immune to chance and unaffected by mood, whose course is merciless regularity, in whose wheels the brain works, sober but not cold, and sense, implacable but not rigid. For only stasis produces coldness, whereas movement, raised by calculation to the limits of the possible, always creates warmth. The weakness of the living, forced to give in to exhausted tissue, is not proof of life—and the durability of iron, a material that isn't subject to fatigue, is no proof of lifelessness. In fact it is the highest form of life, livingness struck from unyielding, equable, steady material. What holds sway in the arena of my triangular railroad junction is the decision of the logical brain, which, to be sure of success, has implanted itself in a body of unconditional certainty: in the body of a machine.

That's why everything human in this metal arena is small and feeble and lost, reduced to an insignificant supporting role in the grand enterprise—just as it is in the abstract world of philosophy and astronomy, the world of clear and great verities. A man in uniform wanders about among bewildering systems of tracks, a tiny human, in this context functioning only as machine. His

significance is no greater than that of a lever, his efficacy no farther reaching than that of a set of points. In this world every
human form of expression counts for less than the mechanical
indication of an instrument. A lever is more important than an
arm, a signal than a gesture. Here it is not the eye that is useful
but the colored light, not the shout but the wailing whistle from
an opened steam vent, here it is not passion that is omnipotent
but regulation and *law*.*

The little house of the guard, the human being, looks like a little toy box. It is all so tiny and inconsequential, whatever he does
in it, whatever happens to him. Irrelevant that he has children
and that they fall ill, that he digs potatoes and feeds his dog, that
his wife scrubs the floors and hangs out the wash. Even the great
tragedies within his soul are lost here, as if they were no more
than minutiae of his existence. His "eternal human" attributes
are—if anything—merely an irritating side effect to his professional functional ones.

Can little heartbeats still make themselves heard where a big
booming one deafens a world? Look at the triangular railroad
junction on a still night, its vale silvered by the light of ten thousand lamps—it is as exalted as the spangled night with stars:
caught in it, as within the glass bell of the atmosphere, are yearn-
ing and satisfaction. It is beginning and stopping-off point, the
introduction to a beautiful and audible future music. The rails
slip and glimmer away—transcontinental hyphens. Their mole-
cules carry the hammering sound waves of distant clattering
wheels, switchmen spring up by the trackside, and signals blos-
som in their lovely luminous green. By the grace of a mathematical system that itself remains concealed, steam escapes, hissing,

---

* Another passage that, to my ear, echoes Rilke in its unreliable fervor.

from opened vents, levers move of their own accord, the miraculous becomes real.

So vast are the dimensions of the new life. That the new art which is to shape it cannot find a form for it is perfectly understandable. The reality is too overwhelming to be adequately represented. A faithful "depiction" is not enough. One would have to feel the heightened and ideal reality of this world, the Platonic ideal of the triangular railroad junction. One would have to affirm its harshness with enthusiasm, see the operation of "Ananke"* in its deadly effects, and prefer destruction by its laws to happiness by the "humane" laws of the sentimental world.

The world to come will be like this triangular railroad junction, raised to some unknown power. The earth has lived through several evolutionary stages—but following always natural laws. It is presently experiencing a new one, which follows constructive, conscious, and no less elemental laws. Regret for the passing of the old forms is like the grief of some antediluvian creature for the disappearance of a prehistoric habitat.

Gray, dusty grasses will sprout shyly between the metal tracks. The "landscape" will acquire a mask of iron.

Frankfurter Zeitung, July 16, 1924

---

* Term from Greek tragedy usually given as "force" or "compulsion," although a line from Sylvia Plath's last poem, "Edge," is perhaps the best rendering: "the illusion of a Greek necessity."

Part V

Berlin Under Construction

16

Skyscrapers
(1922)

For some weeks there has been a fascinating exhibition at the City Hall of designs for large buildings. We hear now that the construction of a skyscraper is to be speeded up. It will be Germany's first.

"Skyscraper" is no technical term, but the popular word for those huge buildings you see in photographs of Manhattan streets. It's a picturesque and rather romantic name. It's the name for a building so tall that its roof, as it were, scratches the sky. There is in the word something of the assertive, revolutionary quality of the builders of Babel.

A skyscraper is the incarnate rebellion against the supposedly unattainable; against the mystery of altitude, against the otherworldliness of the cerulean.

The skyscraper stands at the summit of technical development. It has already overthrown the cold sobriety of "construction," and has begun to approach the romance of nature. The cloud, that remote, wonderful puzzle of creation, God's blessing and curse, two-handed mystery bringing life and destruction, prayed to and dreaded by our ancestors, is now to be made habitable, even cozy. We will make ourselves comfortable among the clouds. We will tell them of the absurdities and the serious things of this world. They will hear the clatter of typewriters and the ringing of telephones, the knocking of central heating, and the dripping of faucets.

It will be a sort of return of the evolved human to the primordial forces of nature. This is an important juncture, and it seems to me we have not paid sufficient attention to it. The building of the first skyscraper is a historical turning point.

WHENEVER I LOOK at pictures of New York, I am filled with awe at the omnipotence of human technology. In this next stage of its development, civilization will have the opportunity to draw nearer to the old notions of culture.

When the steam locomotive was first invented, the poets moaned about the defilement of nature; the imagination predicted terrifying dystopias: whole tracts of the world devoid of grass and trees, rivers dried up, plants withered, butterflies poisoned. They didn't understand that every new development constitutes a mysterious circle, in which the beginning and end touch and become identical.

Because the invention of the airplane was not a declaration of war on winged creatures, quite the opposite: It was fraternization between man and eagle. The earliest miner did not barge his way sacrilegiously into the depths, he returned home to the womb of Mother Nature. What may have the appearance of a war against the elements is in fact union with the elements: man and nature becoming one. There is freedom in skyscrapers as much as on mountaintops.

The long-desired fulfillment of some of the profoundest

wishes of Earth: to overcome shortage of space by elevation and conquest of vertical space. Exploitation of every dimension: exaltation, visible from outside, that also communicates itself to the spirit within.

It is impossible for the proximity of clouds to have no effect on human beings. The view out of the window, taking in the full boundlessness of the horizon, works on both heart and soul. The lungs take in the air of heaven. Clouds wander past the brows of mortal man as previously only around the brows of Olympians.

I can see the skyscraper: a slender, floating construction on its broad pediment, noble and delicate in its lines, whose white and gray sets itself apart from the blue sky. Strong and safe in its assembly, it matches a natural mountain for strength.

Ten thousand people daily flow in and out of it: little office girls, emerging from the tight courtyards of the north of the city, quick tick of heels, black leather handbags swinging, filling elevators, shooting upward like a swarm of swallows.

Men striding out, purpose in their eyes, enterprise in their loose limbs; machine rattle and clatter of conveyances; shouted order of command; the even beat of mechanical perplexity, working toward a common end.

And up above God is disturbed in his everlasting tranquillity, and compelled to take an interest in our tiny destinies.

OH—AND ALREADY you hear that the first skyscraper in Berlin is to contain a great entertainment palace, with cinemas, dance hall, bar, Negro bands, vaudeville, jazz.

Because human nature will not deny its weaknesses, even where it is seemingly in the process of overcoming them.

And if it were possible for us to build a "planet scraper" and to construct settlements on Mars, the expeditions of scientists and engineers would be accompanied by a delegation of bartenders.

I have a shining vision of a bar in the clouds. It's raining champagne cocktails.

Berliner Börsen-Courier, March 12, 1922

17

Architecture

(1929)

It happens from time to time that I fail to distinguish a cabaret from a crematorium, and pass certain scenes actually intended to be amusing, with the quiet shudder that the attributes of death still elicit. Such confusions would not have been possible in previous years. Ugliness, coarseness, and failure could always be brought into some relation to beauty, elegance, and good quality. A building that bore a fleeting, if distressing, resemblance to a classical temple was certain to be a theater for light opera. Something resembling a church was a main railway station. It was embarrassing, but somehow handy. You knew exactly how the deception operated, and never failed to recognize the fake when you saw the true. If you thought you saw marble, you knew you were in the presence of plasterboard. But ever since people have had the idea that modern times needed "modern styles," all the old rules of thumb have stopped helping me. It's as if all the gobbledygook I've learned with so much effort has suddenly been invalidated. It happens from time to time that in my hurry to catch a train I look for a cinema, thinking thereby to find the station. But my method no longer works. The building I took for the station turns out to be a "five o'clock

Redesigning facades on the Kurfürstendamm, 1927.

tea" house in a sports palace. The facades of these modern times are unsettling me.

Still more confusing is interior design. I have learned that those hygienic white operating theaters are actually patisseries. But I continue to mistake those long glass tubes mounted on walls for thermometers. Of course, they are lamps, or as people more correctly say, "sources of illumination." A glass tabletop isn't really there to permit the diner to view his own boots in comfort during a meal, but to help a metal ashtray produce those marrow-piercing, grating sounds when slid across it. There is a class of objects that are wide, white, hard-wearing, deep, and hollow; have no feet; and look like chests. On these, it seems, people sit. Of course they aren't anything as straightforward as chairs, but rather "seating accommodation." Similar confusions are also possible with those living objects collectively referred to as "staff." A girl in red pants and blue jacket with gold buttons, with a round fez on her head, whom—but for the fact that the treachery of these times has begun to dawn on me—I would certainly have taken for a man, but then was foolish enough to take for a sort of royal guard in a costume drama. In fact this girl is in charge of the cloakroom, and of the sales of cigarettes and of those long, slender unjointed silk dolls, who look like merry hanged corpses.

Domestic interior design is a fraught affair. It makes me hanker for the mild and soothing and tasteless red velvet interiors in which people lived so undiscriminatingly no more than twenty years ago. It was unhygienic, dark, cool, probably stuffed full of dangerous bacteria, and pleasant. The amassing of small, useless, fragile, cheap, but tenderly bred knickknacks on the fireplaces and sideboards produced an agreeable contempt that made one feel at home right away. Countering all the tormenting demands of health, windows were kept closed, no noise came up from the street to interrupt the useless and sentimental family conversations. Soft carpets, harboring innumerable dangerous diseases, made life seem livable and even sickness bearable, and in the evenings the vulgar chandeliers spread a gentle, cheerful light that was like a form of happiness.

The lives of our fathers' generation were lived in such poor taste. But their children and grandchildren live in strenuously bracing conditions. Not even nature itself affords as much light and air as some of the new dwellings. For a bedroom there is a glass-walled studio. They dine in gyms. Rooms you would have sworn were tennis courts serve them as libraries and music rooms. Water whooshes in thousands of pipes. They do Swedish exercises in vast aquariums. They relax after meals on white operating tables. And in the evening concealed fluorescent tubes light the room so evenly that it is no longer illuminated, it is a pool of luminosity.

Münchner Illustrierte Presse, October 27, 1929

18

The Very Large Department Store

(1929)

L arge department stores are nothing new in Berlin. But there seemed to be the odd person who bemoaned the lack of a very large department store. Some were not content with the existing four- or five- or six-story department stores, and they dreamed ambitiously of department stores that were to have ten or twelve, or even fifteen stories. It was not part of their plan to be nearer to God—which would have been a futile endeavor in any case—because, on the basis of everything we know, we don't get any nearer to him by climbing up toward the clouds, but if anything perhaps the opposite: the nearer we are to the dust of which we are made. No! The people who dreamed of very large department stores were only out to lift themselves above the smaller department stores, just as with today's runners, one of whom tries to outstrip the other not to reach his target the sooner, but merely to reach some arbitrary mark before the other does. The dreamers of department stores dreamed of a skyscraper. And so one day they built the very large department store, and everyone went along to look at it, and I went with them. . . .

The old, the merely large, department stores are small by comparison, almost like corner shops, even though in its essence

The Karstadt department store on Hermannplatz with swastika flags flying (1939).

there is little to distinguish the very large department store from the merely big ones. It is simply that it has in it more merchandise, more elevators, more shoppers, flights of stairs, escalators, cash registers, salesmen and floorwalkers, uniforms, displays, and cardboard boxes and chests. Of course the merchandise appears to be cheaper. Because where there are so many things close together, they can hardly help not thinking of themselves as precious. In their own eyes they shrink, and they lower their prices, and they become humble, for humility in goods expresses itself as cheapness. And since there are also so many shoppers crowded together, the goods make less of a challenge or an appeal to them; and so they too become humble. If the very large department store looked to begin with like a work of hubris, it comes to seem merely an enormous container for human smallness and modesty: an enormous confession of earthly cheapness.

The escalator seems to me to typify this: It leads us up, by climbing on our behalf. Yes, it doesn't even climb, it flies. Each step carries its shopper aloft, as though afraid he might change his mind. It takes us up to merchandise we might not have bothered to climb an ordinary flight of steps for. Ultimately it makes little difference whether the merchandise is carried down to the waiting shopper, or the shopper is borne up to the waiting merchandise.

The very large department store also has conventional stairs. But they are "newly waxed" and anyone going up them runs the risk of slipping and falling. I think they would like to have dispensed with them altogether, those old-fangled things, that in the context of elevators and escalators seem little better than ladders. To make them appear yet more dangerous, they are newly waxed. Almost unused, they do nothing but carry their own sheer steps aloft. Leftovers from the old days of ruined castles and merely

large department stores—before the advent of the very large kind
we have now.

The very large department store would perhaps have been
built much higher still if it weren't that people believed it
required a roof terrace where the shoppers could eat, drink, look
at the view, and listen to music—and all without getting too cold.
This seems a rather arbitrary belief, as it doesn't seem to be
ingrained in human nature that, following the successful pur-
chase of bed linen, kitchenware, and sports equipment, the shopper should feel the need to drink coffee, eat cake, and listen to
music. But what do I know? Perhaps these requirements are built
into the human character at some deep level. Anyway, it is to
cater to them that the roof garden was built. In the daytime a lot
of people do sit there, eating and drinking, and though it is not
for me to assume that they do so without pleasure, it still looks to
me as if they were merely sitting and drinking to justify the existence of the roof terrace. Yes, even such pleasure as they do
evince may have nothing more than justificatory motives. If the
people themselves, having been borne aloft by the escalators,
were still, even in their diminished mobility, recognizable as
shoppers, then, by the time they got to the roof, they had reached
such a degree of passivity that utterly equated them to merchandise. And even though they pay, still it seems as though they were
paid for. . . .

In complete torpor they are regaled by the sounds of an excellent orchestra. Their eyes take in distant steeples, gasholders, and
horizons. Rare delicacies are offered in such profusion and with
such insistence that their rarity is lost. And just as, within, the
merchandise and the shoppers became modest, so too the delicacies on the roof become modest. Everything is within reach of
anyone. Everyone may aspire to anything.

Therefore the very large department store should not be viewed as a sinful undertaking, as, for example, the Tower of Babel. It is, rather, proof of the inability of the human race of today to be extravagant. It even builds skyscrapers: and the consequence this time isn't a great flood, but just a shop. . . .

Münchner Neueste Nachrichten, September 8, 1929

19

"Stone Berlin"

(1930)

B erlin is a young and unhappy city-in-waiting. There is something fragmentary about its history. Its frequently interrupted, still more frequently diverted or averted develop- ment has been checked and advanced, and by unconscious mis- takes as well as by bad intentions; the many obstacles in its path have, it would seem, helped it to grow. The wickedness, sheer cluelessness, and avarice of its rulers, builders, and protectors draw up the plans, muddle them up again, and confusedly put them into practice. The results—for this city has too many speedily changing aspects for it to be accurate to speak of a single result—are a distressing agglomeration of squares, streets, blocks of tenements, churches, and palaces. A tidy mess, an arbitrariness exactly to plan, a purposeful-seeming aimlessness. Never was so much order thrown at disorder, so much lavishness at parsimony, so much method at madness. If fate can have arbitrariness, then this city has become the nation's capital through a whim of German fate. As if we wanted to prove to the world how much harder it is for us than it is for anyone else! As if there had been one contradictory detail—a capstone—lacking from the structure of our contradictory history! As if we had felt challenged to come

up with an aimlessly sprawling stone emblem for the sorry aimlessness of our national existence! As if we had required one
more proof that we are the most long-suffering of the peoples
of the earth—or, to put it more malignly and medically: the
most masochistic. The story of how absolutism and corruption,
tyranny and speculation, the knout and shabby real estate dealings, cruelty and greed, the pretense of tough law-abidingness
and blathering wheeler-dealing stood shoulder to shoulder, dig-
ging foundations and building streets, and of how ignorance,
poor taste, disaster, bad intentions, and the occasional very rare
happy accident have come together in building the capital of the
German Reich is most fascinatingly told in Werner Hegemann's
book: *Stone Berlin*.

Here in Germany expert understanding tends to go hand in
hand with barely comprehensible jargonizing. Expertise lacks
style, knowledge stammers just as if it were ignorance, and objectivity has no opinions. Werner Hegemann is one of the rare
exceptions (no less German for all that) in whom expert knowledge makes for passion, and passion feeds hunger for knowledge.
Style sharpens his judgment, the facts plead for his opinion—if it
needed a plea—truths underpin his convictions, and a winning
edge of malice sharpens, points, and rounds the writing. This
edge of malice produces something close to a vendetta when the
subject turns to Frederick the Great, whose sobriquet the author
has evidently vowed never to use without encasing it in quotation
marks. He is Werner Hegemann's special enemy. Not since
Voltaire, it seems to me, has Frederick the Great had to suffer
a wittier antagonist. Here is the embodiment of the vengeance
of German literature on the Frenchified Prussian. The present
writer lacks the historical knowledge to refute or uphold the
author's views. He is a "layman," but the "reader" in him would

affirm that the passages of the book he most enjoyed were where Hegemann's stylistic adroitness fed on the weakness of his historical enemy, and where the sharpness of the writing is surely sufficient to make even Frederick's fans admire Hegemann's authorship.

It is, so far as I know, the first successful attempt to follow the stone traces of history in such a way that makes it possible to hear the soft and vanishing tread of the past. Reading it is like looking at someone's testament and hearing it read in the testator's voice. Anecdotes, seemingly merely tossed in, acquire symbolic weight through the way in which they are used and the context in which they appear. The author's near-omniscience in the fields of literature, history, philosophy, and architecture is fused together by his overall historical perspective and his style, so that his "expertise" becomes unobtrusive, and no more than a natural element of his language. The private in the historical is raised to the level of the human, thanks to his fine passion for justice. Passion for justice: That seems to me particularly to characterize this book and its author. With the zeal of the true writer he pursues injustice throughout history, like God following sin through generations still unborn. The striking relevance of the book to today is also rooted in this quality. It is fortunate enough to appear at a time when the scars of the absolutist lash are healing over rapidly, but confusion shows no signs of lessening. The stupidity that is our inheritance and the ignorant snobbery that we have learned from our recent rulers dim and becloud our freedom. Now we have this capital city. Its interests are the same as ours. From its past, for which we are only partly responsible, we ought to learn how to shape its future, for which the whole of Germany is now taking responsibility. *Stone Berlin* (designed and illustrated, by the way, with great beauty and attention to detail) appears just as further damaging scandals are shaking the city and the nation, which seems as yet unaware that Berlin is its chosen representative. From the fact that it has found a historian of this stamp, we ought to acquire confidence that it has a future more wholesome and less warped than its past has been. A city that has had so much knowledge and passion devoted to it surely has a historical mission. It may indeed be young and unhappy, but we may hope it is a city for the future.

Das Tagebuch, July 5, 1930

Part VI

Bourgeoisie and Bohemians

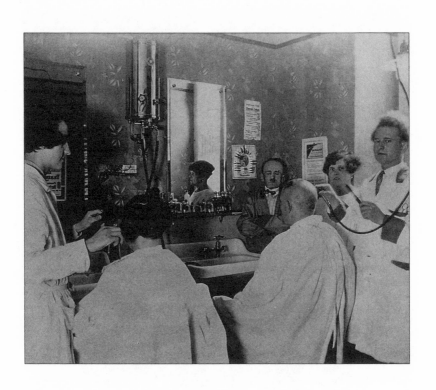

20

The Man in the Barbershop
(1921)

O n Sunday morning there was a stifled, almost canned heat in the barbershop: a desiccated temperature.

Sunlight, split into golden bars by the blinds, bullioned its way into the room. Scissors clacked avidly, and a large fly was buzzing about.

(To date no poet has hymned summer in a barbershop in his iambs. That would be a task worthy of a Theodor Storm, or an Eduard Mörike.* Think of the mild scrape of whetting blade on tautened strop; the soft plashing of soapy water; the flushed cheeks of the apprentices, who—because the master and journeyman are too tired today—don't get their usual smacks: a holiday from discipline!)

But people like to talk at the barber's, even on hot days. And on that particular Sunday morning they were certainly talking a lot.

The man, however, who suddenly crashed into the summery torpor of the barbershop—ginger blond, bull-necked, pugnacious—he talked the most.

No sooner had he slung his hat on the hook, as hard as if he

---

* Novelist and poet Theodor Storm (1817–1888) and lyric poet Eduard Mörike (1804–1875).

wanted to tear it out of the wall, than he was tapping a half-lathered customer on the shoulder, bringing the barber's assistant up short.

What the ginger-haired gentleman talked about was Hamburg.

Entirely without preamble he was off on Hamburg, as though his narrative was nothing but the continuation of a conversation begun on the street.

"The farther north you go, the more nationalist people are. In Hamburg they're really excited about Flag Day. Well, you'll see. It's on its way. Can't be stopped. On, on!"

His sentences grow ever shorter, he rattles subjects together, his words puff out their chests and march: one-two, one-two. It's a nightmare.

And if you—I think—were to go south, or west, or east, it would be just the same. Whichever way you went you'd see people getting more nationalistic. Because what you see is blood.

The ginger-haired gentleman has killed off the summery singsong atmosphere in the barbershop with his crashing sentences. His voice rattles along like a yellow weathervane.

"Will you be joining us, Herr Trischke? Eh! When the time comes? Sure you will! Who wouldn't? And it will come! Mark my words!"

His words rattle, clatter, and bang. Batteries, mortars, rifles, running fire, all come spewing out of his larynx. World wars slumber in his bosom.

Herr Trischke, the barber, would surely have lost a leg—at least!—if he hadn't successfully lathered up the chops of the gentlemen on the General Staff. If war comes he won't go.

But Herr Trischke is silent. Who isn't? Even the fly, buzzing in so summery a fashion a moment ago, now adheres lifelessly to the ceiling, awestruck.

No one speaks, just him, the man. He touched rock bottom,

but he didn't rest; he worked and worked and worked till he had made his way back. He's at the top of the tree now.

One morning not long ago his business partner came up to him and asked him for a loan. And in the afternoon? In the afternoon he was talking to his partner's young wife, and she was wearing a diamond ring!

"You won't catch *my* wife wearing any diamond ring!"

"My wife doesn't own *three* summer hats! *My* sons don't hang around in bars!" And if they *did*, by God—he would knock some sense into them! No matter how old they were! He would knock some sense into them!

He is strict with himself in order to be violent with others. He runs that he may whip others. He fries that others may broil. He wants war so that others may die. He gives up half his hard-earned fortune that others may work.

Oh, he's not a victim of society, he's its beneficiary. Socially and morally he is effective. He does the work of a hundred idle people. He's the go-getting character out of the civics textbook. He puts nothing off till the morrow. His life is a hive of activity, chimney soot, drain smells, sander's hum.

No motor rattle, no belt drive, no clatter of horses' hooves. He is the trench digger, the wire cutter, the whetstone, the insect powder, the coffee machine, the guaranteed-infallible lighter, the dry fuse. Only:

He's my friend from way back. He's the aunt who scoured me every Saturday with a stiff brush. He's the *Kratzbürste.**

My neighbor was a glazier. His wife was a scold. He's my glazier's whining wife.

---

* The German word *Kratzbürste* or "harridan" is used both for the wire brush and the woman wielding it.

Our living room had a clock in it that used to clear its throat before striking the hours. He is that harrumphing.

My schoolmate was at the head of the class, and he had an impeccably neat notebook: The man in the barbershop is the neat notebook of my school friend; my school master's class log; simultaneous equations; a book of logarithms!

He is my headmaster's address at assembly; the kiss of my old-maid aunt; dinner with my guardian; an afternoon in an orphanage; a game of dominoes with my deaf grandfather.

He is duty and decency, sour-smelling and clean.

He isn't a knave: He's a navvy.*

One does run into people like that, in our part of the world, even in midsummer. It feels like encountering a schoolbook in the middle of a suitcase packed for the beach.

And one lives with the idea of summery lassitude and inactivity in the world—green, quiet, almost extinct, the fly buzz, the silent moth flutter, sunshine (broken into bars), the gentle rasping sounds of a razor being stropped, the sleepy blades of the scissors, the soft plashing of soapy water, the tired sleepy chatter of the customers: morning at the barber's, a fit subject for a Storm or a Mörike.

But if he weren't alive, the man, this world would end—this world of whetstones, aunts, logarithm books, pecks on the cheek, knitting needles, school trips.

And of course the world *mustn't* end! . . .

Berliner Börsen-Courier, July 31, 1921

---

* Only *navvy*, the British term for "construction worker" allows a translation that comes close to Roth's style and assonance.

21

Richard Without a Kingdom
(1923)

Richard the Red looks like a king in exile. All he needs is a Shakespeare to build a tragedy around him. He mooches and mopes around: the stuff of drama lacking a dramatist. He sits in other cafés and—oh woe!—is reduced to asking for a newspaper. Richard, formerly the absolute ruler over all printed words, domestic and foreign, turning to other newspaper waiters* for a paper. He, who so to speak enjoyed *droit de seigneur,* the right to deflower the newest editions, now receiving newspapers secondhand! . . .

What?! Do you claim the world no longer knows who Richard is? Richard, the newspaper waiter in the Café des Westens? Richard, who wore his hunchback as a physical sign of intellectual distinction; the crookback as emblem of wisdom and romanticism. His physical defect had the effect of leveling class distinctions, and raised the *waiter* at least into the ranks of the straight-backed newspaper *writers.* In the Romanisches

---

* Many Berlin cafés featured racks of newspapers, domestic and foreign, available at a patron's request; "serving" these was a specific waiter's job, hence "newspaper waiter."

Red Richard. (sketch by Walter Trier)

Café,* the adopted home of Berlin's bohemians, there is a well-grown newspaper waiter. He has all the papers, the *Wiener Journal*, the *Prager Tagblatt*, even the La Plata newspaper. But he doesn't have a hunchback! My gaze slithers down his boring vertiginous back and finds nothing to catch on to.

* A rival establishment, to which Wolfgang Koeppen wrote an exquisite prose ode. It was widely known as "Café Grössenwahn," or "Café Megalomania," and its two rooms, one for celebrities, one for aspirants, were known respectively as "the swimming pool" and "the kiddy pool."

His collection is somehow incomplete. His existence as a literature bearer is not justified in every regard.

Now, Red Richard was different! He had red hair. He was a
special creation of the Almighty's literary advisers, and selected as
newspaper waiter by the PR boss in heaven. He has seen generations of writers come and go. Seen them wind up in prison or on
ministerial chairs. Become revolutionaries and private secre-
taries. And all of them left owing him money. He knew what the
future held for them, he knew the style of their writing, knew
where their pieces had been reprinted, and kept them posted.
Even as he told them, he handed them the paper—it was like getting the news still in its shell. And, if they were obscure or strug-
gling—he helped them. In the glass-fronted cabinet at the Café
des Westens hung, like syntheses in an experimental laboratory,
the products of obscure living persons: a portrait, a poster for
some reading or signing, copies of a new magazine that Richard
hawked around among the clientele. Richard, in fact, was a
patron of the arts.

In the afternoon, if things were quiet, Richard worked on his
memoirs. Those memoirs were never completed. It would appear
that Richard, who always had good taste, finally disdained to
write his memoirs, after so many others had fatuously written
theirs: It was not for him to be mentioned in the same breath as
Ludendorff or Wilhelm.

Admittedly Richard did have one thing in common with all
the memoirists of the postwar period: He too was never in the
war, in the trenches. First they sieved out the tubercular ones—
the hunchbacks' turn was still to come. But if one happened to
ask Richard with a show of surprise why his number hadn't yet
come up, he bent down over the table and breathed his secret:
"You know—just between you and me—I've got—*flat feet.* . . ."

I still remember the painful night when the old Café des Westens closed its doors forever and Richard went around collecting our signatures. That sampling of immortality for his autograph book was the last service he was able to perform for literature. Then Richard vanished, and it took a while before he surfaced in the Romanisches Café. Imagine the pain he felt, returning home as a visitor and an outsider, calling for newspapers instead of distributing them?! . . .

For a while a rumor did the rounds that Richard was going to open a *new* Café des Westens. Nothing would have been more natural. His physical condition, his training, his outlook—all qualified him as an ideal host for modern literature. But nothing happened; Richard did not open another establishment. Half a year later he was forgotten. Not only because people still owed him money; he was forgotten for historical reasons, like a writer who has outlived himself. Richard once had a part in a movie that dealt with the literary milieu of the West End of Berlin. Who knows where that film is playing now? Not once but *twice* Richard's portrait was hung, painted by renowned artists—one of them was König—in the Sezession. Art treated him as a patron merits. Today the portraits are hanging in some chilly drawing room somewhere, where no one has any idea of Richard's character. . . . And a new generation of writers is growing up, without Richard to stand over their cradles. To think that they will never know Red Richard!

One day he showed me a box of butterflies. They were wonderful butterflies and moths, velvety, particolored, red ones and red-and-black and black-and-yellow ones. Someone had invented a process that kept the delicate covering of dead butterflies intact. Richard bought the—as it were—embalmed butterflies to make brooches out of. There are women who will wear insects on their bosoms, I thought. Richard is saved.

A couple of months later, I saw that Richard had a postcard from Leopold Wölfling, the well-known Habsburg archduke. "Dear Richard," the card began. It was the parallel between their historical circumstances that had brought them together. Richard the Red, ex-king, and Leopold Wölfling, ex-prince, were friends. Leopold Wolfling wanted to open a butterfly exhibition in Vienna. But the ladies didn't want butterflies. Brooches are worn on exposed and strategic places—and the lacquered butterfly wings were not well-enough armored to be certain of withstanding an energetic male attack! Now, if Richard had come up with something revealing, say an original form of décolletage, that would have been another matter! But he had offered a barrier instead. The times are not that interested in barriers.

The business did badly, and now Richard is doing badly. But his personal destiny, which in spite of everything seems to put news on his path, chose him of all people to discover Rathenau's murder. Richard happened to be walking along Königsallee, ten minutes after the assassination. He knew just what to do. Richard called the newspapers. If it hadn't been for him, the extra editions could have been delayed by—why, an hour or by even more!

That was the last time Richard made contact with history. Every evening he sits at a little café on the Kurfürstendamm and reads the papers—papers that have passed through others' hands. He is said to own some shares on the stock market. Maybe he is able to live on them. His soul wanders the hunting grounds of the past. Whenever I see him I feel as melancholy as if I had just been looking at an old newspaper, or reading old articles of mine. That's how dear Richard is to me . . .

Neue Berliner Zeitung—12-Uhr-Blatt, January 9, 1923

Bei „Schwanneke"

"At Schwannecke's"

The Word at Schwannecke's
(1928)

Although the noise of the chattering clientele is much more significant than the topics of their chatter, it does finally constitute that type of social and indistinct expression that we refer to as rhubarb. The very particular volume in which people tell each other their news seems to generate all by itself that acoustic chiaroscuro, a sounding murk, in which every communication seems to lose its edges, truth projects the shadow of a lie, and a statement seems to resemble its opposite. And, just as it is difficult to see an object clearly by the light of a harsh but flickering flame, so it is difficult for the man straining his ears to evaluate what he has just heard, particularly—as is most often the case—when it is told him in confidence.

The watering hole for Berlin artists and literary figures—where one can be sure to find at midnight all those who only hours before had sworn that they would never go there again, yes, that they hadn't set foot there for years—houses a class of established bohemian whose creditworthiness is beyond question. None of the clientele really needs to go to bed any later than his bourgeois instincts would tell him to. And each of them, at the end of every evening, promises himself not to go there tomorrow. But the fear that his friends, who are waiting to have a nice talk with him, would say nasty things about him behind his back, prompts him bravely to show his face when it might actually be more courageous to stay away. He comes so as not to disturb the harmony—formed of fear and distrust—of the nooks and corners, and to protect himself and his table mates from the calumnies that are waiting on the lips of those at the next table. If someone had the ability to sit at every table at once, he would hear nothing but good about himself, and yet even such contortions would pale in comparison to those of the others. Still, many approach the very cusp of the miraculous by table-hopping very quickly to keep tabs on what is being said. But even so they fail to match the speed with which those who remain seated change the subject—and, on occasion, their minds as well.

Admittedly there are also some seated customers of such seniority that their rank just about permits them to stand when required, but no longer to visit other tables. Even they are not proof against the fear that somebody somewhere might be saying bad things about them. But they bear the burden of being unpopular as proof of their importance—and these eminences turn the suspicion that less elevated customers are careful to disguise as courtesy into naked contempt and disdain. All the people one doesn't need right now are—for the person who will need them in a year's time—no more than air* which he breathes but doesn't need to see. Softly, softly! Before long they will have roused themselves from their transparent anonymity into that pseudonymous corporality without which it would be impossible to occupy a seat behind an office desk. Those who even today ask for nothing better than to be shadows of bodies will one day cast shadows

* To be "air" to someone in German, *Luft sein*, is a usually terminal snub.

of their own, shadows of patronage over new, anonymous, transparent airy shades. It will fall to them to dole out the movie-reviewing assignments, which today fall into their laps once or twice a year like manna from heaven. They themselves will be participants at conferences they are today sent out to cover, and they will attend premieres sitting next to critics, critics themselves, but representatives of some "new direction," with a new terminology, which will help save them from making judgments and ensure that they stick to prejudices. Therefore it is advisable for cautious spirits not to overlook anyone here, to take in even the least of those present with a certain respect, and to greet the shades in such a way as to suggest that they had the power of speech and were capable of replying. In the long years I have observed the German literary business, I have seen zeroes attach themselves to real numbers, and amount to totals that need to be reckoned with. Yes, a few of the company at Schwannecke's who seemed merely to serve the negligible function of being ornamental vertical lines have become strokes that put paid to the innocent plans of others.* And some illiterates whom one might come upon in the anterooms of editors, trying to spell their way through newspaper headlines, are now all at once reviewing books themselves.

Enmities among the clientele at Schwannecke can also take surprising turns, and it would take a naive person indeed to put his trust in one, and hope to use it, say, for his own advantage. Even after an unmistakable declaration of a so-called ink feud—which, along with the ink vendetta, is about the most dangerous

---

* The German idiom *jemandem einen Strich durch die Rechnung machen* literally refers to drawing a line through a bill, indicating that it has been paid (or cancelled).

custom among the Schwannecke tribes—no one can predict how quickly a feuilleton writer is capable of ending a long-standing campaign against an author that has gone on for days if not weeks. Quite suddenly there is a long and admiring review, without anyone being able to give the how, why, and wherefore. Sources close to both parties have been known to claim that a shared interest in a new type of sports car has brought about a "speedy" reconciliation between the two foes. Because for some time now the mania for speed, with which the construction, destruction, and reconstruction on the Kurfürstendamm and elsewhere has been taking place, seems to have taken hold on the priests of the intellect and their acolytes, and every one of them seems to be capable of forgetting their principles over a fifty-mile-an-hour joyride. The experience of measured speed tearing down the road seems to eclipse for them the sensation of that unmeasured speed with which they forget a commitment. And since, in our contemporary literature, a monocle is a fair stand-in for an eye, it is no longer possible to distinguish sympathy or the lack of it, even in the way ostensible foes regard each other. For which reason I have long made a point of reading personal attacks and diatribes in our literary pages as if they were merely a particular, inverted form of overture.

I have reason too to be irked by the design of Schwannecke's: the long, narrow interior, with square niches stitched along both sides, so that various groups of clients are kept separate from one another, as if they didn't all belong together. I am annoyed by the narrowness of the room, and by the fact that it can't hold everyone who ought to be there. It is one of my favorite fantasies, when I find myself sitting in one of the niches in the early morning, which, here, is an extension of the night. I imagine a colossal, panoptical Schwannecke's with a domed roof, big enough to house all the writers and all the critics, the film producers and their reviewers, the stage and its scribblers, even encompassing the studios and ateliers of individuals who profess the snobbism of a solitude that is not theirs by nature, collapsed and broken-up studies, where only the hammering of a typewriter punctuates the empty thrumming of ideas. I see before me an infinite, as it were hyperreal Schwannecke's, a pantheon of the living—if not live—artistic scene, with room in it too for the garages of the bold poets of speed, and a racetrack for the bards of now, and even a landing strip for the tabloid Homers of aviation.*

Frankfurter Zeitung, June 2, 1928

---

* Tempelhof, Berlin's first airport, received its concession in 1923. The first flights were to Munich and Königsberg.

23

The Kurfürstendamm

(1929)

I n the evening I walk along the Kurfürstendamm. I slink along the walls like a dog. I am on my own, but I have a certain sense that my destiny has me on a leash. From time to time I have to step aside to avoid a fence that has a garden behind it. I am not allowed to set foot there. I envy the streetcars, which are allowed to glide coolly and briskly over the strips of lawn that have been laid in the middle of the thoroughfare. They have been laid expressly for them, as if they were wild animals brought to Berlin from their lush green homes and, like the animals in the Zoologischer Garten, had to be offered a pathetic suggestion of their habitat. Sometimes, instead of a little patch of lawn behind the fence, there's a little gravel patch. Framed by bricks, in a sort of flat distinction, it contains myriad little stones, the sight of which makes one grate one's teeth. I should like to know who the inventor of this stone flora was, and whether the gravel is sprinkled daily so that it doesn't wither and die. Strips of asphalt run parallel to the streetcar lines and lawns, and down these omnibuses and cars clatter, causing traffic jams. Often they enlist the help of traffic lights, which alternate automatically among red, yellow, and green without any visible cause. They are suspended from wires in the air wherever there is a crossroads with one of the side streets—eyes that shine but are sightless. When they are angry they turn red, and when their temper tantrum is over, they turn green once more. When they are red the traffic must stop. Sometimes the traffic lights succeed in turning red just at the right moment, which is to say just as a couple of trucks are coming out of the side street. Mostly though, they lose their temper each time a bicyclist seeks to come out of the side street, or a man pushing a handcart. Even the policemen, who are of course still the representatives of the law, are powerless against the traffic lights on high, the true eyes of the law, compared with which the eyes of the police are just a likeness.

Sometimes the rows of dwellings are interrupted by cafés, cinemas, and theaters. It is to these, really, that the Kurfürstendamm owes its significance as a traffic artery. God knows what it would be without them! That's why they bend all their efforts to add to its greatness. Having heard of its claims to international importance, they try to be international. A restaurant is a little piece of America, a café of France. Of course it looks nothing like New York or Paris, but it awakens a little echo of this or that. In their modesty the places think of themselves as successful copies, but in fact what they are is botched originals. In the American restaurant the menu is in English. I should say that German is the first language of most of the diners, but perhaps their language changes according to their mood and whereabouts.

They don't mind, they can understand a little English. In the French café, they sit out on the terrace, feeling chilly but ever so Parisian. In fact, all the more Parisian for being in Berlin. Evidently because of some police bylaw, the terraces have to be fenced in and set back from the street. Of course this separation distinguishes them from Parisian terraces. But then it is resemblances that are at issue, and not differences. On some terraces a violet light shines, reminiscent of an undertaker's salon. Even so, people are laughing in this light. The collisions between people leaving the terraces, and others entering them, defines the life and the movement of the pedestrians. When they want to cross the street, they go to one of the crossings. If they're in luck, the traffic light will be green, and they will get to the other side, unimpeded, where more café terraces await them.

Trees are planted on the edge of the sidewalk, and newspaper sellers in front of the railings. The news is alarming. The newspapers move faster than the times, not even the cult of speed, for which they are partly responsible, can keep up with them. The afternoon runs panting for the late-evening edition, and the evening chases the first edition of the morning papers. Midnight eyes the threat of the following afternoon, and crosses all its fingers and toes for a printers' strike, which would allow it to behave like midnight for once.

And so the Kurfürstendamm stretches out endlessly day and night. Also, it's being renovated. These two facts need to be emphasized, because of the way it's continually ceding particles of its true self to its designated cultural-historical role. Even though it never stops being "a major traffic artery," it still feels as though it weren't a means to an end but, in all its length, an end in itself. But for the fact that another street takes up where it leaves off, it could have gone on even longer. But even so, its dimensions are appalling enough. Its terrible gift for self-renewal—for "renovating" itself—flies in the face of all natural laws. For a long time I've tried to guess its secret, the quality that enables it to remain itself through all the sudden changes in its physiognomy—yes, to

become still more Kurfürstendamm. It is immutable in its muta-
bility. Its impatience is heroic. Its inconsistency is insistent. A
whimsical piece of whimsy on the part of Creation, you might
say, if you could be sure it was intended.

But unfortunately it seems more likely that it wasn't. . . .

Münchner Neueste Nachrichten, September 29, 1929

Part VII

Berlin's Pleasure Industry

24

The Philosophy of the Panopticum*

(1923)

Currently, in Lindenpassage, there is a historic auction of the last of the Berlin panopticums. A whole world of wax, curiosity, expert copies of life, plastic horror, is being broken up. It was a police report in wax, a three-dimensional *chronique scandaleuse*—and at the same time it immortalized those high points of world history that seemed made for the panoptical form: parades, coronations, five-star pageants. Thanks to a cannily symbolic layout, the Chamber of Horrors was just *one* step away from the Fairy-tale Hall, and the Rulers of Europe a curtain's thickness from the Fun House. It was the revelation of the paradoxical philosophy of the panopticum that earthly grandeur and horror became ridiculous by being given permanence in wax. Never has a memorial industry so stripped its objects of all dignity as the panoptical one. It made monuments without the

---

* The panopticum, or exhibition of (topical) waxworks, was a subject always dear to Roth's heart. The one collection of his feuilletons that was published in his lifetime—in 1928—was called *The Panopticum on Sunday*, and the subject and milieu also made an appearance in *The Tale of the 1002nd Night*, his last completed novel.

pathos of piety. A wax Goethe quite naturally lacks the gravitas of a marble one. The cheap material was able to achieve a lifelike color but not the afflatus of genius. The only achievement of the panopticum was the unintentional ridiculousness with which it atoned for the pathos of this world, and turned it into a kind of Fun House Gallery.

This is because the chief characteristic of the panopticum, its frightening verisimilitude, is finally ridiculous. It is the—actually profoundly unartistic—impulse to produce exterior likeness rather than inner truth: the same impulse as naturalistic photography and the "copy." A wax mass murderer is comical. But a wax Rothschild is also ridiculous. The medium has robbed the one of his gruesomeness and the other of his dignity.

The panopticum has fallen victim to the times, to our awakened pleasure in movement, which expresses itself in the popularity of film. In the age of the movies, the panopticum has no part to play. In an age of intense bustle, rigidity is impossible, even if it attempts to mask its deadness in pedantic lifelikeness. A moving shadow means more to us than a body at rest. We are no longer taken in by a fixed grin. We know that only death has a rictus.

For the very last time the models have a kind of urgency and newsworthiness. The auction is being held—oh, the irony!—in the rooms of the White Mouse. The wax heads are piled up in the anteroom. For practical reasons they have been detached from their bodies, but not completely from the vestiges of their former lives. Here a bearded head has managed to hang on to its cravat, there a shirtfront remains draped around a severed neck. A naked wax girl still smiles, even after her body shattered into pathetic pieces as it was being moved, and the contrast between the smiling lips and the broken body is so gruesomely ironic that for the very first time, a suggestion of grotesque animation

emanates from the figure. It looks as though a mass grave of pre-
served heads had been discovered, a grisly charnel house of dead
life. All these beings lost their heads in the flower of their youth,
it looks as though their souls had been vouchsafed some joyful
experience, and the painful end that overtook them seconds later
had no time to change their expressions. Beside the two hundred
heads living men bargain and haggle, and enormous moving men
drink soup with slurps of satisfaction.

In the room next door are stuffed apes and skeletons of apes,
the dusty booty of popular science that shows only the results and
says nothing about connections and details. Minerals and rare
plants and anthropological bric-a-brac, Indian quivers and spears
and arrows: everything an example of semicivilization and indis-
criminate dabbling, the world of insatiably curious encyclopedia
subscribers, always eager, always wrong. The items provoke a
kind of sentimental contemplation, and they too, like the wax figures, are victims of these times, which create one-sided specialists
in the hope of making people of deep learning, as opposed to
people of broad and general culture.

In the auction room they sell elephant tusks; two men almost
come to blows over a piece of wood carving and a copper vat of
supernatural dimensions, a container from the time of icthyo-
saurs. It is astonishing that a man can spend a hundred million
and more on a single day on a lot of tin, wood, bronze, broken
tables, thrones, and glass cabinets. Watching him, I suddenly
understand the point of this auction: The man is not buying out
of sentiment. He is, rather, an exemplar of the new times, in a
short fur coat, cigar jammed between metal teeth, all calm and
calculating: a schemer, a man working his percentages, confident
of victory. God knows what his hands will make of those pots and
plates and carvings, how the horrid monsters will change in his

storehouses. Twentieth-century man can turn ducats out of all sorts of trash.

Which is really the higher purpose of the panopticum.

The gold maker of our time, the modern alchemist, makes capital out of the sensation of the past. He finds the stone of wisdom—not by experimenting but by speculation—in every medieval cooking pot. Whatever he touches appreciates.

So there he stands, victor over the ephemeral world, gold maker, highest bidder, all-purchaser. His spacious girth has room for an entire panopticum, pots and pans, spears and apes, murderers and princes, the grotesque and the trivial. He swallows it all up—the ultimate redeemer of panoptical existence.

Berliner Börsen Courier, February 25, 1923

25

An Hour at the Amusement Park
(1924)

Spring in Berlin received its official sanction as a season of merriment (*Amüsemang*),* with the opening of the enormous Luna Park, just beyond the Halensee Bridge, set by the God of sensations at the very end of the Kurfürstendamm, which seems like one never-ending promise of sensations. Here the fun becomes insane, the absurdity hyperbolic, the jollification both strenuous and harmless. There are infernal machines that cause bitter sweat before they rouse any joys: a deranged pyramid that tries to top its own summit. Undemanding fun becomes its own caricature. How strange that someone trying to have a good time will walk up an uncertain jazz band staircase, get stuck halfway up, unable to go up or down, and instead of laughing, finds himself laughed at by everyone else!

The whole purpose of this grotesque machine is to expose the person who entrusted himself to its mercy in his full inadequacy. The point of the other amusements is the same. Woe betide him

---

* This spelling accurately reflects the *echt Berlinisch* mispronunciation of Frederick the Great's beloved French—especially of words ending in -*ent* and -*ant* (as in *Restaurang*).

Roller coaster in Luna Park, 1928.

who breaches the circumference of the "Devil's Wheel"! The
good fellow will walk out onto a round arena, and look back over
his shoulder with a smile. Suddenly the signal will sound, what
was solid becomes flimsy, what was secure uneasy, the floor spins,
bodies collide into one another, outstretched arms vainly seek for
somewhere to grip in this suddenly deranged world of violent
spinning. You may reach for the barriers, but they too are spinning, the coattails of the man next to you are flying out, the cane
propped on the quaking ground is shaken free of one's trembling
grasp, a savage draft seizes you by the neck and hurls you cen-
turies back. You will land somewhere in the Stone Age! Never yet
has such furious movement brought in its train such slowness in

the passage of time. Everything is spinning, only time stands still. The rotation goes on forever. And when the wheel finally stops spinning, the riders in their relief forget that they have paid money to enjoy themselves, and only had the fright of their lives. They feel glad to have gotten out alive.

See the Tin Lake! Its metal waves coil endlessly, the pushing and lifting force of hidden engines creates swells and calms, heights and troughs. You sit in your boat and think the gentle rhythm of the water will rock you a little. Then a wave rears up and makes straight for you. You struggle against it, without leaving the spot, till an expert knocks your boat forward with a contemptuous shove. The energy you expended would have sufficed to see you through a real storm at sea.

Someone tries to cover a round target with six flat rubber disks. He throws one after another, hoping to win himself a wristwatch. The desire to win impels his arm, the fear of losing holds it back, and his excited consciousness, the seat of prudence and of frivolity, wavers between the will to throw and the trembling arm. Meanwhile any jewelery store would offer him the same "guaranteed 100 percent Swiss watch" for the same money and with no exertion or risk.

The enjoyment here is in the mockery of human endeavor. I watch a gentleman shattering the crockery in the "China store" by flinging hard rubber balls at it. He isn't aware that the sounds of breakage are what prompt him to new efforts, he throws one ball after another, he hasn't noticed that a number of people are clustering around, watching him. Maybe they have some terrible glimmering of the truth, and the question whether this devastation might be the meaning of life, is stillborn on their lips. . . .

Frankfurter Zeitung, May 16, 1924

26

The Twelfth Berlin
Six-Day Races
(1925)

As I write, the eager cyclists have already covered more than eight hundred miles, without having gone anywhere. They don't even want to get anywhere! They go around and around the same track, which is two hundred meters long and a million meters boring. If this track had a finish line, then you could say there was a prize waiting for them at the end, for which it was worth putting themselves through six days of torment. The track has no finish line, but still there is a prize for the riders: That's the type of silly, childish thoughts I have as I watch the race. There are only another hundred hours to go. If I stayed here, my face would get to look like the megaphone by which the crowd in this madhouse is from time to time fed bits of information. Astonishing, really, that they still look human. They ought to look like megaphones, like screams, like brutal desires, like beery ecstasies, like bicycles, like blind wants, like decadent barbarism. But the unconscious drive to remain in God's image seems to be so strong in humans that not even the six-day races can quite eradicate it. They still look human, even at the end of six days of racing, or of watching the races. On the sixth day God created man, so that man might race for six days. It was worth it.

It's a Saturday night. Packed buses race through the streets headed for the Kaiserdamm. There are a hundred policemen. At the turnstiles the people press—there really isn't a comparison, I should have to say—like people trying to get into the six-day races. At eight o'clock the megaphone announced that there were no more tickets. There are resigned people, turning back around, quiet, sad, their heads hanging. They are inconsolable. That's the way souls look as the gates of heaven are banged shut in front in their metaphorical faces. Whole families head for home. Men with crying infants in their arms. Men who seem close to tears themselves. Oh! Where can they go now? Six days they have worked, and every evening, before going to sleep, they have sworn to others and to themselves that on the Saturday they would definitely go to the six-day races. What's left for them? Suicide, at best! But even experienced suicides will insist that their own death is much less exciting than one of Huschke's "breaks."

Enough of those unhappy ones! Let's turn our attention instead to those prudent souls who four days ago locked up their homes and set off with backpacks, subtenants, grandchildren, dogs, parrots, and canaries to the Kaiserdamm, to set up house there. They have brought with them everything the police have said it is illegal to bring. Their pets are in the rucksacks, occasionally betraying their presence with pathetic cries for help, directed at a public that is not inclined to betray its humanity by any sort of sympathy. The moment a tormented dog yelps here, he sounds like one of the humans anyway. All the way around the steep walls, faces, faces, faces. The rows are like shelves, head is pressed alongside head, like the spines of books in a great library. Sometimes you get a notion you might take down one or another of them from its place, between finger and thumb. But you'd be wrong. The heads are mounted on bodies, and the bodies are glued—glued by excitement and sweat—to their seats. Ten thousand throats emit a wild cry, a single cry, that drowns out the more evolved yelp of any barking dog. Down there a rider has "broken." What a sensation!

Painful, the deathly white of the floodlights, great lamps as hard and heartless as suns in the underworld, glacial suns, spreading an atmosphere of polar festiveness. The shine of the lights drives you toward the cloakroom. Just where the cone of light cuts into the shadow with a razor-sharp edge, millions of particles of dust are busy. When the crowd cries out, there is a commotion among them: tumult, terror, chaos among the placid Brownian floating and drifting of the dust particles. So violent is the effect on the atmosphere. Sometimes the dust storm of ecstasy is enough to throw the packed human ranks into disorder as well. Shrill women's cries (giving the lie to the expression "weaker sex") whirl furiously into the massed basses of men's voices, and it is like being given a firsthand experience of the Furies. At the same time a conscientious housewife unpacks some long-stored piece of cheese from the editorial page of her newspaper, and there is a whiff of food and politics. The smell sinks, beaten down by the gravid air, hangs above the heads of those sitting below like a louring cloud, and they look up, suspiciously, furiously, as though they could see the smell and kill it with their eyes. Somebody cracks a joke, a whole row laughs, one witticism sets off another, and, like matches, they flare up and burn down.

Policemen hold on to pillars, occasionally even, when there is no honest citizen around, on to the backs of pickpockets, for a sight of the track. So far is the majesty of the state lowered by the enthusiasm of the population. It's impossible to spot the plainclothesmen, not even with their regulation rubber collars on. They could really achieve something here—if only they were still up to it! If a burglar managed to get to the racetrack, it would be like a sanctuary for him. Thirsty people pull bottles of schnapps out of their pockets and offer their neighbors a drink. People behave humanely, as during a shared calamity. Someone who has left his seat to answer a call that is even more irresistible than the lure of the six-day races returns to find his place taken. Then human kindness turns into its opposite, and there is a bout of fisticuffs between the two pretenders. The great excitement holds thousands of little excitements.

Down below, on the mirror-smooth track, the riders go around, backs parallel to the ground, around and around and around. Hour after hour, mile after mile. Push pedals, right and left, break, get left behind, ahead of you another man, steel and rubber, a shirt, dripping sweat, all round you the crowd, at the end of six days a prize, a bath, a long rest, a photographer, flashbulbs, a woman, champagne, a trip somewhere, a write-up in a sports paper. At the end of six days is life, which exists for you because you've just raced for six days, and so that you can race another six days. You're not yet dead, but you're still waiting to enter life. Listen to the trumpet, the six days of judgment are at hand, the megaphone announcing a prize for winning a section of the race, awarded by a patron who's feeling bored, and doesn't want to have come here for nothing. He has things to do later, his chauffeur is freezing outside, clapping his hands to stay warm. So: Let's put up a small prize to give the lazy fellows a kick up the behind, get them to show a bit of life! They show a bit of life.

It's past midnight; a sleepy little girl, some sports fan's offspring, is crying in a whiny little voice, her wailing has trouble clearing a little path for itself through the dirty airwaves:* A

---

* Another bit of Rilkean physics.

minor acoustic tragedy is at hand. A drunkard is reeling around in the background, and his tongue struggles with the language, obstinately and bitterly, for a whole hour. People tell him to pipe down. He can't. Whatever is bothering him has to be told. A few are asleep and snoring. Their noses rattle loudly and rhythmically, like little carts laden with old iron, on narrow tracks. In balconies and boxes bald heads gleam like round mirrors. What, precisely, is the relationship between capital and hair loss?

Dawn is about to break. No inkling of the new day will be seen in here. Here the icy suns of the underworld will continue to shine, the wheels will turn, the drunks will sober up, the sleepers awaken—while, outside, the world will shake off the night and the fog will slink away from the fields, and the wintry sun, red and slow, will begin its journey. The leftovers of four days and a hundred families waft through the arena.

Outside the drivers are asleep. A part of the rain of money that's pouring down within will drip onto them as well. They've been waiting for it. One lot lives off the other. That's the way it goes.

Frankfurter Zeitung, January 20, 1925

27

The Conversion of a Sinner in Berlin's UFA Palace*

(1925)

In the newspapers, but also on a hundred bright and arresting posters, I saw advertisements for America's funniest comedy, guaranteeing me a rip-roaring evening's entertainment. There was a gold-braided porter standing in front of the three lofty gates, and funny announcements of the film and a very famous clown's face in red and yellow. A great swarm of happy people pressed up to the box office and bought tickets for themselves. Nothing betrayed the deep seriousness that awaited me inside the theater, and I had no idea what shocks my poor impious soul would encounter there. . . .

I had long ago set aside the habit of seeing in every Berlin mosque a Muhammadan house of worship. I knew that the mosques here are movie theaters, and the Orient is a movie. Many years ago, once, in the days when I was still a believer, I wanted to attend an early mass. I stepped into the church—and

---

* UFA (Universum Film Aktien Gesellschaft), Germany's leading film production company from 1917, had connections with MGM and Paramount, whose films it distributed in Germany as well as its own. The UFA Palace was a movie theater with more than two thousand seats, and a seventy-five-member orchestra.

found myself in a railway station. Later on I learned that architectural style counts for nothing, and that it is in red-brick warehouses equipped with lightning conductors that the altar is set up, and God's word is heard. . . .

But this time was different:

I was sitting in the third row in front of the green velvet curtain. Suddenly the hall darkened, the curtain slowly parted, and a mysterious light that could not have been created by God, and that nature couldn't manage in a thousand years, ran in soft rivulets over the silvery walls of the hall and down the front of the stage. It was as though a waterfall had been slowly tamed—housetrained— in the course of many years and then applied to the walls of this palace, to run down them slowly and civilly, made to answer to human needs, elemental forces with pretty manners, forces of nature that had had a good talking-to. This illumination was compounded of dawn light and evening red, of empyrean clarity and infernal haze, of big-city air and sylvan green, of moonshine and midnight sun. Things that nature can only accomplish separately or in succession, were here encompassed in the one hall and in one minute. And thus it was clear to me that an unknown and powerful godhead was here at play, if not in earnest. There was not room to fall to my knees, because we were sitting packed together, but, if it's possible to say so: It was as though my knees fell to their knees. . . .

All around me, so far as one can tell faith from people's faces, were members of various creeds. All were moved. And when a young black man started to pray at an organ, and the mighty sounds of the divine instrument filled the opened hearts of those present, it grew so quiet in the hall that in all the building one could hear nothing but the breathing of the people, almost as at a medical examination, on the order: Breathe deeply! . . .

Then a little silver bell tinkled, and out of habit I lowered my head, and, like a small boy, peeked between my fingers. I saw the curtain break in two, and from the opening black men dripped one by one down the steps off the stage, men bearing musical instruments. Last of all, in a great rush, like a teacher entering a classroom, a slender bespectacled young man jumped into the orchestra pit, his long hair flying in front of him in the wind he himself had caused.

He was the conductor. . . .

And it was wonderful to behold him as he gesticulated wildly with his arms, how he fenced with the whole orchestra with his swift baton, nettled the violins, and elicited stern growls of protest from the double bass, shook the sails of the timpani, and drew silvery snakes from the flutes—and, lo, the name of it was Offenbach.

As the music weighed light or heavy, the projection changed its colors from blue to red to yellow, the musicians were ghosts, and the conductor's hair sometimes burned with a sacred fire up to the ceiling. The domestic waterfalls still flowed. And finally our reverence discharged itself in violent applause, and those who applauded the loudest were the agnostics. We all confessed the will of a supernatural power, a metaphysical theater management, a heavenly industry. . . .

And then the projectionist began to officiate at the film by Harold Lloyd.* But who was there who could laugh? No mirth shook my diaphragm. My thoughts were on death, the grave, and the hereafter. And even as the man on the screen was performing some wonderful comic gag, I decided I would dedicate the rest of my life to God, and become a hermit.

At the end of the show I quickly rushed away into a deep dark forest, which I have not left since. . . .

Frankfurter Zeitung, November 19, 1925

---

* The Harold Lloyd film (not) discussed here is *The Freshman*.

28

The Berlin Pleasure Industry
(1930)

Sometimes, in a fit of incurable melancholy, I go into one of the standard Berlin nightclubs, not to cheer myself up, you understand, but to take malicious pleasure at the phenomenon of so much industrialized merriment. Any anxiety that it might be my advancing years that make me incapable of enjoying myself is quickly allayed by my perfectly objective view of the indescribable monotony of international nightlife. The entire mechanism by which fun is produced and communicated these days seems ever more simplistic and transparent the more human nature is forced to import entertainment from outside. It's as though that crude force that seems capable almost of making something out of nothing had now been tried out on people's spirits and feelings, in the attempt to create capital from our inborn inclination and need for amusement. And it's as though this crude and homogenized purveying of fun had also succeeded in producing in all the cities of the world one standardized type of night owl, with the same set of strictly normed and basic requirements, which can be satisfied in accordance with one or two simple rules. At around two o'clock at night, anyway, the image given by a bar, a "luxury spot," "a dance hall," is one and the same in Berlin, Paris, Marseilles, and Cairo:

the perfumed smoke of international "luxury brand" cigarettes hangs under the ceiling like a sort of gaseous lining or underpinning. The soft reddish illumination works not to create light but to suppress it. The glowing colors of the cocktails, mixed in accordance with international recipes, evoke semiprecious stones in liquid form and are poured into curved glass bowls about the size of a coconut half. Stiff yellow bundles of straws stick out of metal holders, the only remote memory of a long-gone rustic period of human history.

In the corner the band is installed, not to sit but to perform incessant and foolish movements that remind one of the exercise "marching in place." Merely switched to the world of bacchic militarism from that of war, the saxophone—profane trump of a profane, so to speak, penultimate judgment—flashes and gleams, moans and wails, yelps and croons. The musicians do not wear jackets. They sit in their shirtsleeves like bowlers, in sports shirts like tennis players, in that relaxed Anglo-Saxon uniform that seems to suggest that the production of sound and noise is more a sporting vocation than an artistic one. Bar girls all over the world are made out of the same substance of beauty, with little concession to the local variations of climate, geology, and race, poured equally over every country by a prodigally lavish godhead, to produce that international, slender, narrow-hipped type of child-woman in whom vice is paired with training, knee-jerk modernity with traditional seduction-by-helplessness, active and passive suffrage with the willingness to be bought. In every city there is the prototypical young, or rather, ageless, player in male dress (this the only overt indication of its sex): smooth features and slicked-back hair, padded shoulders and compressed hips, baggy, billowing pants and pointed patent leather boots—and the casual demeanor out of fashion magazines, the nonchalance of a window dummy, the fake worldweariness in the glassy stare, and the thin lips touched up by nature itself in homage, of course, to certain photographic originals. Couples get up simultaneously and indifferently to do their athletic dance movements. The movements of the musicians are livelier than those of the dancers. It's as though the marionette-like movements of the musicians had taken all the life out of the dancers. The couples who, under the heading "classic modern dance," go from city to city earning their daily/nightly bread with the same mechanical smile that consists only of the baring of brilliantly maintained teeth—they at least produce an imitation of life. There is no owner to be seen any-where, as if these bars didn't actually belong to anyone, as if they were institutions of public luxury, just as buses and streetlights are institutions of utility, as though the entertainment industry wanted to prove its close relationship to the utility industry.

In a city like Berlin there are stock companies that are capable of satisfying the entertainment needs of several social classes at once, catering to the "cosmopolite" in the West End, providing "solid bourgeois" pleasures in other parts of the city, and in a third supplying that part of the lower middle class that wants to have some inkling of the "grand monde" with its very own "third-class establishments." And just as in a department store there are clothes and food for every social class and even for the myriad delicate nuances in between, carefully graded by price and "quality," so the great names of the pleasure industry supply every class with the appropriate entertainment and the appropri-ate—and affordable—drink, from champagne and cocktails to cognac to kirsch to sweet liqueurs down to Patzenhofer beer. In the course of a single night, in which my mournfulness was such that it compelled me to experience the pain of every class of big-city dweller athirst for joy, I slowly made the rounds from the bars of the West End of Berlin to those of the Friedrichstrasse, and from there to the bars in the north of the city, finishing up in the drinking places that are frequented by the so-called lumpenproletariat. As I went, I noticed the schnapps getting stronger, the beers lighter and brighter, the wines more acidic, the music cheaper, and the women older and stouter. Yes, I had the sensation that somewhere there was some merciless force or organization—a commercial undertaking, of course—that implacably forced the whole population to nocturnal pleasures, as it were belaboring it with joys, while husbanding the raw material with extreme care, down to the very last scrap. Saxophonists who have lost their wind playing in the classy bars of the West End carry on playing to the middle class till they lose their hearing, and then they wind up in proletarian dives. Dancers start out reed thin, to slip slowly, in the fullness of time and their bodies, in accordance with a strict plan, down from the zones of prodigality to those where people keep count, to the third where people save their pennies, to the very lowest finally, where the expenditure of money is either an accident or a calamity.

One of these places—it was already far along in years, a hoary ancient among the clubs of Berlin—was celebrating its fiftieth anniversary, and was giving out detailed anniversary programs, complete with unobtainable photographs of long-gone vaudeville stars and popular favorites and a "historical look back." From this it appeared that the establishment, having once been founded and run by a single man, has fallen into the numerous hands of a consortium, a consortium, I like to imagine, of deadly serious fellows, heavyweight fat cats. There is the photograph of the founding father: the broad round face of a man who knew to live and let live, with the twinkling eyes of a connoisseur, with a mighty upturned moustache betraying a kind of martial good humor, and a slow smile that legitimates the man's unquestioned desire for profit.

There follow pictures of the "famous numbers," the "diseuses," a race of courageous women setting foot on the stage as on a battlefield, armored in corsets, in long skirts, under which peep out— flirtatiously, seductively, sinfully—snow white or salmon pink stockings and tightly laced dancing shoes, Boadiceas with bare throats and powerful shoulders and with abundant piled-up hair on their heads, such that a little nodding double-entendre can't have been an easy matter; and finally the dancers with round, shapely legs, sewn, one would think, into the whirling expanse of ruffled and lacy underskirts, loose girls of sweet harmlessness and easy virtue. Yes, that's the way it was then. The clubowner walked around among the tables, and nodded and smiled and allowed his patrons to live and encouraged them to sin as hard as they could. The jokes were terrible, but the people were cheerful, the women were very dressed, but at least they were flesh and blood, and not the product of hygienic training. Pleasure was always a business, but at least it wasn't yet an industry.

Münchner Neueste Nachrichten, May 1, 1930

Part VIII

An Apolitical Observer Goes to the Reichstag

Der Leichenzug des Reichspräsidenten Ebert vor dem Reichstag.

29

The Tour Around the Victory Column

(1921)

T he sky has got itself all blued up, as though it were going to get its picture taken, and the March sun is friendly and eager to please. The Victory Column* soars up into the azure, naked and slender, as though sunbathing. Following the law that governs the popularity of all outstanding personalities, it has now, following its accident, attained the level of popularity that only failed assassinations may confer.

For many years it was neglected and lonely. Street photographers with long-legged flamingoesque equipment liked to use it as a free backdrop for the vacant smiles of their human subjects. It was a little knickknack of German history, something that appeared on picture postcards for tourists, a nice destination for school outings. No grown-ups or locals would dream of going up it.

But now, at lunchtime, two or three hundred Berliners stand

---

* The "Siegessäule" was built to commemorate Prussian victories in the nine-teenth century (most important, those over Austria in 1866 and France in 1871), and originally stood directly in front of the Reichstag. In 1938 it was moved to its present location by the Nazis.

around the Victory Column, sniffing what's left of an averted calamity, and politicizing.

I know for a fact that the gentleman in the cape and the broad-brimmed hat, who looks like a giant mushroom that's sprouted somewhere in the shadiest depths of the Tiergarten, is a private scholar, working on such matters as the crystallization of quartz. For a quarter of a century, he's had the habit of taking his daily walk on a particular avenue, back and forth, with the regularity of a brass pendulum, and then home again. But today, see! He only walked once up the avenue, and then made straight for the Victory Column. And here he is, listening with interest to the disquisition of a little fellow who's standing hat in hand and mopping his bald head with a blue-bordered handkerchief, about picric acid.

I don't know whether picric acid comes into quartz crystallography or not. But the interest taken in it by the quartz expert seems positively boundless.

"Dynamite"—I hear—"is dangerous stuff. You use dynamite to blast tunnels. It's even more dangerous on account of it's kept in cardboard boxes."

"What amazes me is that no one smelled the fuse right away!" observes a lady. "When I'm at home, I can tell if anything's burning." The lady sniffs as though some trace of the fuse might still be lingering in the air. All the other women sniff along with her, and duly agree: "Ooh, yes!"

"What's with this picnic stuff anyway?" a nearby colossus asks me. A pink tinge suffuses his face, as though he were just gazing into an Alpine sunset. His picnic has cheered him up as if it were some mass entertainment.

A nationalist says it must have been a communist. A communist pops up and says that he suspects the nationalists. An argument breaks out, and the whiff of a party-political wrangle stinks up to high heaven.

Meanwhile the Victory Column soars blithely and insouciantly straight up into the air, and is pleased to have been put off-limits to visitors.

And I firmly believe: If I could go up the Victory Column now, I would hear the Almighty laughing at the folly and wickedness of this world, which lives by political parties and dies by picric acid.

Neue Berliner-Zeitung—12-Uhr-Blatt, March 15, 1921

30

A Visit to the Rathenau
Museum
(1924)

I'm sorry to say that the Rathenau* Museum is not open to the general public. To inspect the house on Königsallee, you will need a pass from the keeper of paintings. Foreign visitors on the whole don't want to put themselves to the trouble of visiting government premises in Berlin, even though I have to say that the Office of the Keeper of Paintings in the Interior Ministry is more of a humane institution than an official one, an oasis, in fact, of humanity in a desert of bureaucracy. A "Rathenau Society" is "in the process of formation"—in other words: Such a thing will one day come about. Once it exists it may be possible to visit Rathenau's house without the necessity for a prior detour to the ministry. For the most part it is foreigners who want to see where the man—who died so terribly—lived.

He lived wonderfully. Among great books and rare objects, amid beautiful paintings and colors, with useless, sublime, tiny, fragile, impressive, tenderness-eliciting, powerful, dreamy things;

---

* Rathenau was the serving foreign minister at the time of his death, a German Jewish politician murdered by right-wing militants. The character "Arnhem" in Musil's *Man Without Qualities* is supposed to be modeled on him.

surrounded by evidence of the human past, of human wisdom, human beauty, human strength, and human suffering: by the breath of the eternal human. That is what makes outlandish things seem familiar and foreign things at home here. Even the downright "exotic" doesn't dazzle, doesn't overpower, confuse, or startle. Its surprise is gently administered. Distancing things extend an invitation. Intimate things are discreet. A loving hand has instinctively created order here. Following hidden inner laws, a prophetic eye has searched. A brilliantly imaginative pedantry has had its way here, classifying and bringing together. Everything here—the books, the cabinets, the tables—is lovingly and indulgently allowed the secret rhythm of its natural being.

The house is an organic whole, wisely divided into above and below: the upstairs with bedroom and bathroom, guest room, and small private study and the more professional, more official downstairs, where there is also the main study, the desk of the man in public life (the one upstairs is that of the private citizen and writer—I almost said: poet). Everywhere there are the books, the symbols of this life: Tieck, Ariosto, Kant, Chesterfield, Plutarch, Goethe. The list could be extended indefinitely. There is almost no name in the great and unending history of literature that is not represented here. Among significant modern and contemporary authors, very few are missing. Two bookcases are filled with volumes that were sent to Rathenau with respectful, humble, polite, fervent requests and dedications. So rich and unstinting was his contact with the creative and productive brains of the epoch that a stream of intellectual labor made its way into his house, as if following a natural law.

Again and again, one runs into the book of books, the Bible. Old Bibles of inestimable bibliophilic value, showpieces of the collection. Small, handy editions of the New Testament in places that bespeak their fond and frequent use: on the desk and by the bed. There is a New Testament with the Greek text and Luther's translation. Rathenau compared the translation with the original, noted points of difference, sprinkled astonished and quietly plangent question marks in the margin. Discrepancies are shot down with discreet little arrows, the texts are treated roughly as a military strategist would treat his field of operations on a General Staff map. He campaigned with thoughts, put errors to flight, surrounded them, conquered new worlds and distant works, allied himself with lasting powers. He was like a peaceful commander of the intellect; with love for the little beauties of daily life, the ornamental culture of domesticity. Upstairs, on his own, his very own personal walls, he hung pictures that he'd painted himself, the works of a writer who liked to dabble in other arts. He never visited a foreign city without going to its antique shops. He sorted the grain from the chaff. His servant tells stories of how he once gazed at an old chest of drawers, and, in a sudden inspiration, instructed him to remove the metal adornments on the locks. "They don't belong!" They were taken off, and under the metal there were facings of ivory. So visionary was his eye.

And yet it couldn't see his end approaching. On his desk upstairs I saw a book called: *German Youth and the Needs of the Hour.* Oh, he always overestimated that part of German youth whose victim he was to be. In one room, on *one* table, in peaceful and significant proximity I found the wise old *Shulchan Aruch*, the religious rule book of Diaspora Orthodoxy, and the old *Weissenfelsische Songbook.**

---

* A compendium of Jewish rules and practices from the sixteenth century. The *Weissenfelsische Songbook* is a collection of some six hundred German hymns.

Pervading the house and the being of this man was the spirit of conciliation. His life is characterized by its attempt to bring together antiquity, Judaism, and early Christianity. A strong chord of conciliation is sounded in the books he read and those he wrote. It was the effort to bring the various instruments of different cultural worlds within the ambit of a single orchestra. By day he read and studied the New Testament. It lay beside his bed to fill him with its love. He was a Christian; you won't find a better one.

He made a simple man, released him from the ignorance and want that people fall into through poverty and bad background. How many great writers could make the same claim?

He was his servant, today a state-employed guide in the Rathenau House, and a work of the deceased, a living witness to his goodness and efficacy. I want to print his name here: He is Hermann Merkel, from East Prussia. He has been a servant half his life, and in Rathenau's house he became a fine, quiet, and thoughtful man.

"Do you read these books sometimes?" I asked him. "Yes," he said. "I don't understand everything in them. But I think to myself: Even if a man doesn't understand everything—at least reading won't make him any more stupid."

Rathenau's servant talks in *aperçus*.

As I'm writing these pages, a man comes to call on me, a friend who is going through a bad time—and not just today. He sees that I'm writing about Rathenau, and he tells me: "Four years ago I wrote to him. He gave me a recommendation to the AEG.* But they didn't have any work at the time. So he sent me four hundred marks." "Did you know him?" "No! I wrote to him out of the blue. An old professor of mine suggested I do so."

* Allgemeine Elektrizitäts Gesellschaft (General Electric Company).

A stranger writes a letter to a stranger. The good man hears the lament of his brother from the depths. He will have heard many laments, and helped.

I walk past the place where he met his end. It is not true that a murder is just a murder. This one here was a thousandfold murder, not to be forgotten or avenged.

Frankfurter Zeitung, June 24, 1924

31

Election Campaign in Berlin

(1924)

The cold, clinical rhythm of this city is immune to "election fever." So what if the billboards blazon out the parties' slogans, the willfully inflated promises, the catchpenny philosophies, the phrases and metaphors couched in colorful images. I didn't see one single person with the patience, the time, and the curiosity to read one of these proclamations—not one who didn't let the leaflet he had just been handed flutter away. Maybe it takes a particularly dramatic and suggestive image to penetrate the consciousness of these people for whom only work exists, and pleasure. Maybe these fanatics of objectivity, of precision, of antifanaticism are so fixed in their political convictions that no rushed campaign mounted in a single week—consisting of slogans and billboards, speeches and posters—can persuade them. The candid observer is obliged to note, incidentally, that none of the party election machines works with one-tenth of the wit and resourcefulness that are employed by the advertising and PR departments of dozens of factories, businesses, stores, and fashion designers.

The sober bureaucracy of Berlin election propaganda (irrespective of party) confines itself to the old and unsuccessful means. It prints long communications on gray fibrous paper in small type (italic, as a rule, too) that present a curious typographical image. But with this vertiginous waste of words, not one manages to leap forth in the form of an arresting, compelling, bone-freezing optical shout. However many parties there are and however hard some of them try to brand the others as "un-German," this type of propaganda proves how German they *all* are. How alien to all of them are the rowdy means of true effectiveness. How, with honest naïveté and a minute scrutiny of the fundamentals, they all seek to persuade the reader—and all they do is bore him. Even in their exaggerations they remain shy. Even in their lies, timorous. They work with the heavy and pathetic weaponry of ethics—made in Germany. No flames lick the walls. No shouts ring from the billboards. The announcements of music halls, movies, the promotion of cigarettes, the fervor of business advertising—their nightly blaze above the roofs of Potsdamer Platz—drown, suffocate, and obliterate any of the political battle cries in an inferno of light and noise and color. The machinery of this half-Americanized city remains clinical and performs its myriad sober functions without passion, without being brushed by even a whiff of political conflict.

I read in the Berlin tabloids desperate efforts by the main editorial writers to describe the "election campaign." It's as if they had a powerful telescope through which they viewed the phases and manifestations of the election—and then turned it around to view everything else. In this way they take upon themselves some of the work of the various party offices (admittedly, of all the parties equally), and blow up the confrontations into global conflicts. Anyone who reads their accounts and doesn't know the city would think there were Wild West–style shoot-outs between the various orators and poster campaigns. In fact it's not like that at all. A few youths sneak around at night on "glue patrols," tearing down posters and putting up others. But it takes a trained eye to spot them among the crowds of sneaking pimps, gussied-up whores, love-hungry pedestrians, and reeling drunks. The business of pleasure, the tireless, well-oiled machinery of thrills, "*Amüsemangs*," gambling clubs, and naked dancers, leaves the voter with precious few resources. It's only in the market in the mornings that I heard women talking politics with their shopping bags; in among the vegetable stands the cut and thrust of campaigning. The markets are the electoral battlefields of Berlin: I have to say so in the interest of truth.

Admittedly, on Potsdamer Platz, a little forest of papers* has been planted. Its young trunks have such names as *Völkischer Ratgeber, Kampfbund, Deutscher Ring, Deutsches Tageblatt*, and they are equipped with the inevitable swastikas, which are carved deep into all bark nowadays, on the branches of sentences, in among black-white-red phraseology. On spongy banks of editorials the bluish buttonhole flowers of Scout movements and *Wandervögel*† grow rampant. Here the roving eye will look in vain for a clearing of common sense. The heavily mossed trunks won't allow even the merest puff of wit to pass. You find yourself stumbling through ungrammatical, antigrammatical undergrowth. Solecisms flower and thrive in the yawning gulches of the lead articles. You hear the repetitive *hack-hack-hack* of the nationalist woodpecker.

But these newspapers find only sellers. I am their sole buyer.

---

* Literally, a forest of leaves, the expression for "the products of the press," a *Blatt* being a newspaper as well as a leaf. The whole paragraph is an extended play on this analogy.

† The Wandervogel (or "ramblers") movement began in turn-of-the century Germany.

Only on Sundays do you come across political scout troops with sandals, walking sticks, and knives. In the woods they do round dances, they rave about nature, and have big brawls with each other. It's a strange, baffling young generation. It covets the poet's eye in a fine frenzy rolling, but not his shy piety and love of nature. You see them at railway stations, the blooming, wheat-blond girls, born to be mothers, but turning into political Furies. They wear shapeless windbreakers, full skirts, and short haircuts. They have unnaturally long strides and absurdly mannish gestures, but nature takes its revenge on them, because as soon as they shout out their "*Heil!*" or their "Yech!" their voices take on the repellent shrieking edge of hysteria.

Frankfurter Zeitung, April 29, 1924

32

An Apolitical Observer Goes to the Reichstag

(1924)

The location of the German parliament is symbolic. Only Königsplatz separates the Reichstag building from the Tiergarten's green pastoral. The apolitical observer is sorry to lose the fine May morning on which the new German Reichstag first meets.

The great edifice will be thirty years old in December. It has irritated people of taste and democratic inclinations for the better part of three decades now. Over its entrance is inscribed the dedication: *"Dem deutschen Volke"* (To the German people). But on its dome, seventy-five meters above street level, is a huge golden crown, a massive weight, completely out of scale with the dome, and utterly at variance with the dedication.

One could be forgiven for thinking this was the front entrance to the building—for assuming that the magnificent facade with the six great Corinthian pillars is there to greet the representatives of the German people, a little pompously, perhaps, but with dignity. But this front entrance isn't. The great doors are kept locked. They opened just once in the time of the republic—for Rathenau's funeral. The stoutness of the six Corinthian pillars goes unrewarded. The facade is only for show. The front part of

Beer party for Reichstag members, 1925.

the Reichstag gives the impression of a vast mansion whose owners are away. Barefoot German youth plays on the steps. A green
policeman sprouts like an ornamental palm—a lonely bit of green
in that arid waste of stone.

It's to the side, through a small tradesmen's entrance on
Simsonstrasse, that the representatives of the people betake
themselves to their work. It's impossible *not* to see this as a symbolic leftover from the times of Kaiser Wilhelm II. Bronze casts
of four German emperors stand in the entrance hall, as though to
review the parade of delegates. The plenary room, grave and
dark, paneled in brown wood, has little enclosures for members
of the press and public—uncomfortable, unwelcoming, con-
stricted, constricting.

Today, on the opening day of the Reichstag, they have been

packed since two o'clock. The ushers take a ceremonially sharpened view of proceedings. Special correspondents interested in personalities and atmosphere hang around the corridors hoping to catch Ludendorff's* arrival. The politically and vulgarly curious are there as well. Their breath is shallow and rapid. Gentlemen caress their damp pates with old-fashioned handkerchiefs. Ladies, related to the gentlemen who will appear today, take off their gloves to use them as fans. Only the public is not in the space provided for it. It has failed to take advantage of the favorable situation of its enclosure, which permits its visitors to stand above the parties. No one takes advantage of this favorable circumstance.

One would have expected the atmosphere to be a little festive, at least as festive as for the opening of some exhibition toward which the whole nation, irrespective of party, has been working. Even those delegates—thinks our apolitical observer—who are opposed to parliamentary democracy, should feel some respect, if not for it then at least for their own role, which they are about to begin to play. Perhaps the ceremonial, the useful uniform of every formal situation, should be sterner and more elaborate. Democratic institutions are bad at ceremony, but it gives the drifting participant at least a little distraction from his own drift and his desire to draw attention to himself, and keeps him quiet in spite of himself. A dignified person will gain composure. It deepens quiet and stifles noise. It would force this body of men, which is put together from

---

* World War I general (1865–1937), who, like the slightly better known Hindenburg, despite losing the war, somehow retained his personal popularity during the twenties, and figured in right-wing Nationalist politics. Ultimately Hitler made monkeys of them both.

opposites, to be quiet if only for a couple of hours, into one form of common purpose which is silence.

Here, though, in the German Reichstag, each party has not only its own political convictions but also its own ritual. There is no sense of overall decorum. Foreign ambassadors—the stately Lord d'Abernon,* for instance—are sitting in the box. The eyes of America, France, and Italy are directed at the representatives of the German people. And what do they see? The goose-stepping of the nationalists. Wrangling among the communists. Ludendorff in dark glasses. The apolitical observer cannot understand why, more than any other professional grouping in the world, German politicians are so driven to make asses of themselves, before they've even embarked on their politics, which are a further reservoir of asininity. But then, what does the apolitical observer understand of the mysteries of politics?

The seventy-nine-year-old veteran president, who has a weak voice, receives a call from the right to "Speak up!" That boorish intervention—doesn't it have a familiar ring to it? Wasn't it at a cabaret, where a gentleman, remembering what he'd paid for admission and having ordered up a bottle of wine, called out to the emcee, "Speak up!!!" in such a way that the three exclamation marks, or better—indignation marks—were clearly visible? Oh— and where have I heard that whistling coming from the communist benches? It was in high school, wasn't it, in my junior year! Is it that I've outgrown it because I'm apolitical?

The man who provoked this storm of whistling was General Ludendorff. The last time I saw him, we were both, he and I, still at war. We both came out on the losing side. Since then our paths

* The British Ambassador to Germany from 1920 to 1926.

have separated. He became a politician, and I didn't. No one gave me any medals or decorations, even though I lost as well. Now I have the opportunity to view him in civilian clothes. There is a certain round amiability about his waistcoat and his double chin, which is supposed to inspire confidence. Why does everyone shout when he gets up? He's changed. He's older, slower, more settled and middle class. Perhaps he always was just a middle-class man in heroic garb. There's not much about him of Mars, god of war.

Now they're singing "The Internationale" on my left and "Deutschland über Alles" on my right. Simultaneously, as if it didn't make more sense to sing them consecutively. Why not have music, my friends? Why shouldn't politicians sing? Why will the one not hear the other out? Isn't it possible that both songs have something to be said for them? In some respects Germany really is above other countries. And in other ways internationalism isn't the worst. We apolitical observers know what we owe the world, and what we've given it. Why don't the politicians know?

While they're still singing in the plenary room, I walk down the empty corridors. I see a large library, the Reichstag library. It could be called "Book Room" if they wanted to avoid the very common "library." And what is it called? It's called "book depot."* Well, let's go into the book depot anyway! We find precious volumes on all subjects, but also kitschy allegorical statues, ponderous virtues hewn from rock. The library should be called a virtue depot. Majestic overload wherever you look. Most un-Prussian-kingly prodigality with the material; reheated

---

* *Bücherspeicher*, an ugly word that Goebbels would have been proud of.

tradition without innovation; show without warmth; frozen displays of pomp. How should humanity, understanding, compassion, exist here? In the "dome room" there is a chandelier that weighs eight metric tons—as heavy as the fate of the people who own the chandelier. They've shelled out twenty-six and a half million marks for their Reichstag. It looks imposing, no doubt about it. It would be nice if the delegates made it impressive as well.

Frankfurter Zeitung, May 30, 1924

33

Farewell to the Dead

(1925)

Today republican Berlin bade farewell to the dead president of the German Reich.* This city, so heartless in its bustle, so cold in its evident urge to utility, and so often teetering on the edge of kitsch where it would be sensitive—just today this city wore a hurt, even a tragic expression on its face. In every street the cortege passed through there was silence. Silence moved the veiled lights of the candelabra, and it was as though silence were the sole force that was moving the people—as if they weren't walking but were slowly being pushed along by silence.

In the morning Wilhelmstrasse was thronged with people. But not animated, no! Because there was a somber mood among them, even where there was no formal mourning. Wilhelmstrasse is blocked off. There are obelisks, erect, frozen, black guards standing at the entrance to the blocked-off part of it; exotic ornaments, fetched from afar and planted on the tarmac. Even so they don't look out of place. They make one forget it was ever a street. The thoroughfare, the passage, the public street is suddenly reduced to

---

* Friedrich Ebert, (1871–1925), the leader of the Social Democratic Party, and president of the Weimar Republic from 1919 to 1925.

President Ebert's funeral cortege outside the Reichstag.

a tragically beautiful courtyard. Obelisks, dark evergreen, dark in their durability—they turn that most living of human institutions, the street—into the stillest and most immutable: a cemetery.

There is the courtyard of the house. Resting along the walls are wreaths with colored ribbons, like visitors who have come a long way, and are tired. A few steps have decked themselves in thin black crepe. Suddenly they are not steps anymore that you climb to gain access to a house. They are signposts of grief. You pass up these steps, you don't climb them. In the first room there are wreaths propped against the wall, waiting. People as they pass bend down to read what is written on the ribbons. It looks like a visitor greeting another visitor.

On the table lies a book for visitors to write their names. An ordinary book, quite small, bound in green cloth, a neutral sort of prop. After all, it only contains names. A lot of names, moving in their simplicity, names of ordinary people: Franz Kruleweit, innkeeper; Frieda Beckmann, guesthouse manager; Arnold Krug, war veteran; Robert Weitig, carpenter. Did they come so that they could say they had once been inside the house of the president of the Reich? Out of curiosity, making the most of the occasion? And maybe they *were* just curious when they set out. But by the time they wrote out their good, simple names, I am sure they were moved. Because they are simple people. It is easier for grief to find its way into the hearts of such people. They are not guarded by bitter skepticism.

It is an easy thing to feel moved in this house. The Reich's keeper of paintings, Redslob, and the director, Jessner, have turned the small, relatively low-ceilinged rooms into spaces that elude conventional measurement. The walls are all draped in fine black cloth. The veiled mirrors are learning to live without light. It is no longer their purpose to reflect life, but to absorb death, to hide it in their silver surface, that is capable of producing so much depth. Colorful paintings mute their tones behind veils. Walls, corners, and ceilings seem to flow into one another in one softened, edgeless blackness. Only the candles that stand at either side of the bier are bare and uncovered, and the two honor guards. Their stillness softens the good, calming, golden light. There are gold chairs for the visitors. They seem no longer to be made of bright metal. It's as though the chairs were carved from the yellow candlelight. Their splendor is undeniable, but grievously reinforced and simultaneously softened.

Outside, more and more people are now filing past the house. Confused carriages turn away, automobiles slow down, the closer they come, people pack together, treading on one another's heels, shoulder to shoulder.

A memorial service for the dead man is held at twelve noon in the State Opera House on Königsplatz for the schoolchildren of Berlin. The orchestra of the State Opera plays Mozart's K.477.* Max von Schillings conducts. The National and Cathedral Choirs sing under their choirmaster Professor Hugo Rudel. On either side of the stage are members of the government, seated on two rows of chairs. The Minister for Education, Arts, and Sciences, Professor Dr. Becker, addresses the young listeners. He reads a surprisingly well-written speech, objective for all its dignity, and interesting to follow in spite of its heavy use of stock phrases. The minister is a professor. To go by his speech (which was a sort of confession), not a born democrat, but one made from his understanding of the historical circumstances. He refers to the United States, where political struggle is every bit as intense as it is here, and where the death of a historical personage is nevertheless sufficient to silence the day-to-day arguments. He explains the difference between Bismarck's centralized and authoritarian state and the ideal of antiquity: the *res publica*. He lends his support to the latter, and calls on his young audience to support it likewise. It is a politically significant speech, more democratic than one would have expected from such a man, and therefore thrice welcome. Marx† says a few words. Then the orchestra plays the Adagio from Bruckner's Seventh Symphony. The hall is full of young people, pupils and students, and teachers of all ages. All those sitting here probably have some political affiliation. Many are probably on the far right, a long way from their education minister. And yet this ceremony must have made some impression on them. It would be nice to have a few more democratic ceremonies like this for teachers and students, without the melancholy occasion.

---

* The Masonic Funeral Music.
† The then chancellor, Wilhelm Marx.

At one o'clock the streets of the city center are filled with a hurried dignity. People are trotting off somewhere or other, then just stop. Anxious automobiles are desperately looking for a way out. Heavy trucks roll slowly by. Coachmen stand up on their boxes and let their horses go where they will. Around the Reichstag everyone is pressed together, twelve deep, behind blue cordons of police. Anyone hoping to get into the Reichstag has to be pulled out by the police past eight pairs of shoulders. If you look out from the platform at the front of the Reichstag onto the expanse of Königsplatz, you see one enormous field of swaying faces. It's as though the faces and the invisible bodies grew out of the ground, out of the lawn, and perhaps one could pluck some of these people. Above them are red and multicolored flags. They flower and unfurl. Policemen and soldiers stand around like leaden shapes: a watchful fence around an endless garden of humanity.

The Potsdam Station is no longer a station, no longer a gateway to the world, but a gateway to death. One descends black steps. Put away behind black cloths are all the noisy, merry sounds of a traveling, jingling, calling, tooting world. Signals are asleep, silent in silent corners. Do any trains still depart from here? Are there still such things as ticket counters, lights, red and green signals, switchmen? The waiting room has become an anteroom to eternity.

Outside, off to one side, where you can already make out the city streets, waits the hearse, all green on the inside with pine branches. It is an ordinary truck. Companies of men once sat in such trucks and rolled into the open arms of death. The truck bears a factual, undignified, meaningless number on its chest. It has been shrouded in black. Now the number looks like the black-bordered name of a mourner.

Outside the station the coffin stands on a catafalque. Incense is burning on both sides. The fragrance rises. Pine twigs have been spread over the paving stones, and muffle the stride of passersby. The coffin is all on its own, without any honor guard; given over to the street, the city, the people. No one guards it. The Reich flag is spread large and luminously over the coffin. It's the visual equivalent of a farewell speech. You see it, and you understand what it says.

It grows dark. Life jingles, toots, and hammers. The coffin has disappeared. Travelers hurry in and out of the station. You hear the shout of a newspaper vendor. For the first time in years, piety—respect—has been more audible than the city's normal clamor.

Frankfurter Zeitung, March 5, 1925

Part IX

Look Back in Anger

34

The Auto-da-Fé of the Mind

(1933)

Very few observers anywhere in the world seem to have understood what the Third Reich's burning of books, the expulsion of Jewish writers, and all its other crazy assaults on the intellect actually mean. The technical apotheosis of the barbarians, the terrible march of the mechanized orangutans, armed with hand grenades, poison gas, ammonia, and nitroglycerine, with gas masks and airplanes, the return of the spiritual (if not the actual) descendants of the Cimbri and Teutoni—all this means far more than the threatened and terrorized world seems to realize: It must be understood. Let me say it loud and clear: The European mind is capitulating. It is capitulating out of weakness, out of sloth, out of apathy, out of lack of imagination (it will be the task of some future generation to establish the reasons for this disgraceful capitulation).

Now, as the smoke of our burned books rises into the sky, we German writers of Jewish descent must acknowledge above all that we have been defeated. Let us, who were fighting on the front line, under the banner of the European mind, let us fulfill the noblest duty of the defeated warrior: Let us concede our defeat.

Yes, we have been beaten.

Now is not the time to reach for the laurels that will one day be ours. It would be childish to predict the ultimate victory of the human spirit over the rampant denizens of the Leuna-Werke, the "I.G. Farbenwerke"* and other chemical and industrial giants. We are proud of our defeat. We stood in the front row of the defenders of Europe, and we were the first to be defeated. Our comrades "of Aryan descent" can still hope to be pardoned (always assuming that they will be prepared to make some concession to the language of Goebbels and Göring). There is even a chance that the vandals of the Third Reich will try to exploit such "Aryan" writers of great renown as Thomas Mann and Gerhart Hauptmann (currently per-secuted) for a while, in order to trick mankind into believing that National Socialism has some respect for the human spirit. But we writers of Jewish descent are, thank God, safe from any temptation to take the side of the barbarians in any way. We are the only repre-sentatives of Europe who are debarred from returning to Germany. Even if there were in our ranks a traitor, who, from personal ambi-tion, stupidity, and blindness, wanted to conclude a shameful peace with the destroyers of Europe—he couldn't do it! That "Asiatic" and "Oriental" blood which the current wielders of power in the German Reich hold against us will quite certainly not permit us to desert from the noble ranks of the European army. God himself— and we are proud of the fact—will not allow us to betray Europe, Christendom, and Judaism. God is with the vanquished, not with

* Two enormous—and, in the case of I.G. Farben, notorious—German petro-chemical concerns. The organization of industries into enormous monoliths was one of the developments that attended the rise of Hitler. But even before that, Gustav Stresemann, the Weimar foreign minister for most of the mid-twenties, observed: "Without I.G. and coal, I could have no foreign policy."

the victors! At a time when His Holiness, the infallible Pope of Christendom, is concluding a peace agreement, a Concordat, with the enemies of Christ, when the Protestants are establishing a "German church" and censoring the Bible, we descendants of the old Jews, the forefathers of European culture, are the only legitimate German representatives of that culture. Thanks to inscrutable divine wisdom, we are physically incapable of betraying it to the heathen civilization of poison gases, to the ammonia-breathing Germanic war god.

Have German writers of Jewish extraction—or for that matter German writers—ever felt at home in the German Reich? There is a justifiable sense that German authors, of Jewish or non-Jewish origins, have at all times been strangers in Germany, immigrants on home ground, consumed with longing for their real fatherland even when they were within its borders. From the time that Bismarck's Second Reich gave physical, materialist, and military forces precedence over the life of the intellect, when the character of the drill sergeant was proposed and recognized by the world as the typical representative of Germany, from that time German writers have felt they were living in moral banishment and exile. Behind the sergeant stood the engineer who supplied him with weapons, the chemist who brewed poison gas to destroy the human brain, and at the same time formulated the drug to relieve his migraine; the German professor, falsely depicted in German humorous satirical magazines as an absent-minded dreamer who forgets his umbrella, but who is in fact the most dangerous (the most dogmatic) enemy of European civilization: the inventor of the philological equivalent of poison gas, who is paid to disseminate the idea of Prussian superiority, the non-commissioned officer of the university, which in the time of Wilhelm II became a barracks.

In the new German Reich the only free and independent people, the only revolutionaries in the proper sense, were the writers. Which is why, long before the advent of Hitler, they felt themselves to be émigrés and expatriates in that empire of technology, of corporals, of parades, and of standing at attention. If you want to understand the burning of the books, you must understand that the current Third Reich is a logical extension of the Prussian empire of Bismarck and the Hohenzollerns, and not any sort of reaction to the poor German republic with its feeble German Democrats and Social Democrats. Prussia, the ruler of Germany, was always an enemy of the intellect, of books, of the Book of Books—that is, the Bible—of Jews and Christians, of humanism and Europe. Hitler's Third Reich is only so alarming to the rest of Europe because it sets itself to put into action what was always the Prussian project anyway: to burn the books, to murder the Jews, and to revise Christianity.

The great historical error of the younger generation in Germany was that it subjected itself to the Prussian drill sergeant, instead of joining forces with the German intellect. About 1900 Jews started to appear in Germany who were classified as "Kaiser Wilhelm's Jews," or "Jewish Prussians," or "Jewish lieutenants of the reserve," or even "Sunday Jews." Without setting aside their religion, they tried to transform it into a kind of Protestantism, and their temples into Prussian barracks. They referred to themselves as "German citizens of the Jewish faith" and the fact that they chose the term "German citizens" instead of merely "Germans" goes to show that they themselves sensed that citizenship was a different category from people and nation. They had just about enough willpower not to repudiate the thousand-year-old tradition of their forefathers, but they lacked the strength not to falsify this tradition. Because they didn't have the courage to convert, *they* *preferred instead to have the entire Jewish religion baptized.* The result was Jewish priests with a Protestant bearing and in Protestant costume; "Reformed Israelite communities" that worshiped on Sundays instead of the Sabbath; Jews who had themselves driven to temple—the house of a betrayed God—on Yom Kippur in luxurious carriages, dressed in the uniforms of Prussian lieutenants of the reserve; Jews who eventually came to view the "Jewish confession" as a state-authorized concession to Jehovah as a kind of twin of the Prussian god. . . . They felt entitled to take out a lease on "German civilization"; inconstant and fickle as they were, to introduce and to support literary and other "fashions"; undiscriminating as they had become, *novarum rerum cupidissimi,* * to admire every version of corruption in literature, in the visual arts, in the theater, because they had forgotten Jehovah; to profess liberalism and freethinking.

It would be true to say that, from about 1900, German cultural life was largely defined, if not dominated by this "top class" of German Jews. To be fair, what they did was not wholly bad. Even their errors were sometimes salutary. In the whole of that large kingdom with a population of sixty million, among all those industrialists, there was—individual exceptions aside—no class that was actively interested in art and intellect. As far as the Prussian Junkers are concerned, the civilized world will know that they were just about able to read and write. One of their representatives, President Hindenburg, openly admitted *that he had never read a book in his life.* And, incidentally, it was this icon, ancient from early youth, that the workers, Social Democrats, journalists, artists, and Jews worshipped during the war, and that the German people (workers, Jews, journalists, artists, Social Democrats, and the

* "very desirous of new things," besotted with the new and the fashionable.

rest of them) then reelected president. Is a people that elects as its president an icon that has never read a book all that far away from burning books itself? And are the Jewish writers, scholars, and philosophers who voted for Hindenburg really entitled to complain about the bonfire in which our thoughts are consumed?

As for the industrialists—their minds were taken up by iron and steel, by guns and "Big Berthas"; they were smelting the modern version of "Siegfried's sword." The big businesspeople were producing the cheap junk labeled "Made in Germany" with which they flooded an unhappy world. *Only the German Jews (doctors, lawyers, tradesmen, department store owners, artisans, or manufacturers) were interested in books, theater, museums, music.* Even if they were occasionally guilty of bad taste, it remains a fact that there was no one else in the whole of Germany capable of pointing out and correcting their errors. The magazines and newspapers were edited by Jews, managed by Jews, read by Jews! A swarm of intellectual Jewish critics and reviewers discovered and promoted numerous "pure Aryan" poets, writers, and actors! Does there exist—now that theater and literature have been "cleansed"—a single outstanding actor or writer who was not recognized and praised at a time when reviewing and public opinion were in the hands of Jews? I challenge the Third Reich to come up with a single example of a gifted "pure Aryan" poet, actor, or musician who was kept down by the Jews and emancipated by Herr Goebbels! It's only the feeblest dilettantes who flourish in the swastika's shadow, in the bloody glow cast by the ash heaps in which we are consumed. . . .

From the beginning of the twentieth century, the following writers—Jews, half Jews, and quarter Jews ("of Semitic origin," to adopt the parlance of the Third Reich)—have made their contribution to German literature!

The Viennese Peter Altenberg, a twentieth-century troubadour, a sensitive singer of female elegance and beauty, long vilified as a "decadent pornographer" by the barbarians of racial theory; Oscar Blumenthal, the author of clever comedies without any grandeur but full of taste; Richard Beer-Hoffmann, a noble makar of German, an inheritor and interpreter of the biblical tradition; Max Brod, the selfless friend of Franz Kafka, a storyteller from a great tradition, full of zest and erudition, who brought back to life the great figure of Tycho Brahe; Alfred Döblin, the writer whose contribution to German literature was the character of the lower-class Berliner, one of the most original creations of the intellectual world; Bruno Frank, a conscientious wielder of words, an experienced playwright, pacifist, and singer of Prussia's history; Ludwig Fulda, a lyric poet and author of comedies full of charm and wit; the tireless Maximilian Harden, perhaps the only authentic German man of letters; Walter Hasenclever, one of the most intense dramatists; Georg Hermann, a plain and truthful novelist of the petit bourgeoisie; Paul Heyse (half Jew), the first German Nobel laureate; Hugo von Hofmannsthal, one of the noblest writers in verse and prose, the classical heir to the Catholic treasures of old Austria; Alfred Kerr, a theater reviewer of abundant imagination; Karl Kraus, the great polemicist, a master of German letters, a fanatical purist of language, an almost unassailable apostle of style; Else Lasker-Schüler, a poet: what need of an epithet, the word itself is enough; Klaus Mann (half Jew, the son of Thomas Mann), a promising young novelist, with considerable stylistic gifts; Alfred and Robert Neumann, impressive epic writers both; Rainer Maria Rilke (quarter Jew), one of the greatest European poets; Peter Panter, a witty firework of a polemicist; Carl Sternheim, one of the most acute writers of prose and drama; Ernst Toller, the poet of *The Swallow Book*, a revolutionary dramatist, who, for love of the freedom of the German people spent seven years in a Bavarian fortress;

Jakob Wassermann, one of the leading European novelists; Franz
Werfel, a lyrical playwright and novelist, and a wonderful poet; Karl
Wolfskehl, a great and noble rewriter of myths; Carl Zuckmayer, a
powerful dramatist; Arnold Zweig, the author of the splendid
Sergeant Grisha and *De Vriendt's homecoming*, an inspired novelist
and essayist. An inadequate and incomplete listing of those soldiers
of the intellect who were defeated by the Third Reich! The reader
doesn't need to take note of each individual name. It is enough if he
salutes them, them and other Jewish writers who are among my
closest friends, and whom friendship forbids me to label: Stefan
Zweig, Hermann Kesten, Egon Erwin Kisch, Ernst Weiss, Alfred
Polgar, Walter Mehring, Siegfried Kracauer, Valeriu Marcu, Lion
Feuchtwanger, the deceased Hermann Ungar and the revered seer
and prophet, Max Picard.

I hope other German Jewish writers not on my list will forgive
me for having omitted them. May those who do appear not be
offended by finding their names next to those of some enemy or
rival. They have all fallen on the intellect's field of honor. All of
them, in the eyes of the German murderer and arsonist, share a
common fault: *their Jewish blood and their European intellect.*

The threatened and terrorized world must understand that the
arrival on the scene of Corporal Hitler does not mark the beginning of any new chapter in the history of anti-Semitism: Far from
it! What the arsonists tell us is true, though not in the way they
intended: This Third Reich is only the beginning of the end! By
destroying Jews they are persecuting Christ. For the first time
the Jews are not being murdered for crucifying Christ but for
having produced him from their midst. If the books of Jewish or
supposed Jewish authors are burned, what is really set fire to is
the Book of Books: the Bible. If Jewish judges and attorneys are
expelled or locked up, it represents a symbolic assault on law and

justice. If authors with European reputations are exiled, it is a way of proclaiming one's contempt for France and Britain. If communists are tortured, it carries the fight to the Russian and Slavic world, which is always far more that of Tolstoy and Dostoyevsky than that of Lenin and Trotsky. By making Austria a laughingstock, it makes a mockery of German Catholicism; and if one sets out to conquer or annex it, that is a threat to the whole of the Adriatic. Mussolini is mistaken; he has failed to understand his Cimbri and Teutoni; ages ago another Roman allowed himself similarly to be taken in by barbarians: Mussolini should have studied his Roman history more closely! By making up to the fascists, one shows one's contempt for "Roman law." One day the world will realize with astonishment that it was conquered by a corporal (albeit one who already had a field marshal to do his bidding!). We German writers of Jewish extraction are the first to have been vanquished for Europe. We at least are not guilty of blindness or falsehood. All we have is honor . . .!

The great gain to German literature from Jewish writers is the theme of the city. Jews have discovered and written about the urban scene and the spiritual landscape of the city dweller. They have revealed the whole diversity of urban civilisation. They have discovered the café and the factory, the bar and the hotel, Berlin's bourgeoisie and its banks, the watering holes of the rich and the slums of the poor, sin and vice, the day of the city and the city by night, the character of the inhabitant of the metropolis. This theme was almost imposed on the gifted Jewish writers by the urban milieu from which most of them came, to which their parents had been forced to move, and also by their more highly evolved sensibility and their Jewish aptitude for cosmopolitanism. The majority of non-Jewish German writers concentrated on the description of the rural landscapes that to them were home. In Germany, more than any other country, there is a "folk literature" based on region, landscape, tribe, often of high literary value, but necessarily inaccessible to a wider European public. As far as "abroad" was concerned, there was only that "Germany" *whose literary mouthpieces were predominantly Jewish writers.* It is through them that the French, the English, the American reader gain their sense of German reality. But this precisely is the basis for further accusations from narrow-minded nationalists and historians against Jewish writers. In the most infantile and jejeune manner, they took the subject matter, the setting, for the author's personal character. A Jewish writer was "remote from the soil" when he wrote about the city; a "café house writer" when he discovered bars; a "traitor to the fatherland" when he depicted the world; a "superficial scribbler" when he found more sensual forms than the dry, abstract language of the German provincial dilettante; a "feuilletonist" if he happened to have charm and lightness of touch; a "joker" if he was witty; and if he happened to take on the description of the countryside, it was straightway objected that "he saw with his head and not his heart." Jakob Wassermann's moving testimonial, *My Career as a German and a Jew,* was vilified; it was forgotten that the one and only German war song was written by an Austrian Jew who died on the battlefield, Lieutnant H. Zuckermann. They forgot the patriotic poems of Ernst Lissauer; they repudiated the Rhenish dramas of the half Jewish Zuckmayer, so popular with the theatergoing public.

Literary anti-Semitism has existed in Germany since 1900. The racist anti-Semite Adolf Barthels, the moderate anti-Semite Paul Fechter, and many others attack the literary works of Jewish writers, often with personal invective. Certainly coarse and tasteless individuals may also be found among Jewish scribblers. But it is always these who are offered as the typical representatives of the Jewish writer! As early as 1918, before putting a book on display in their windows, provincial bookshop owners would ask if an author was Jewish—not even bothering to read it. And never— even though literary anti-Semitism was growing ever more viru- lent—did a Jewish author say anything publicly against it. There are strong and deep friendships between German Jewish writers and the best of the non-Jewish writers. A fine German stylist like Hans Carossa (not a Jew) was discovered and promoted by an admirable Jewish writer (though not one who wants to be named in this context). Let us remind our readers that Hans Carossa was *the only non-Jewish German writer* who refused to belong to the academy of the "Third Reich." The German press was silent about this refusal, so nothing is known about it abroad either.

Many of us served in the war, many died. We have written for Germany, we have died for Germany. We have spilled our blood for Germany in two ways: the blood that runs in our veins, and the blood with which we write. We have sung Germany, the real Germany! And that is why today we are being burned by Germany!

Cahiers Juifs (Paris), September/November 1933

(from the French)

Credits and Sources

Archive of the Editors: 84, 116, 136, 140

Archiv Ernst Thormann, Berlin: 40

Archiv Abraham Pisarek: 22

Bildarchiv PreuBischer Kulturbesitz, Berlin: 83, 94, 124, 177

Bundesarchiv Koblenz: 62

Deutshes Historisches Museum, Berlin: 182

Kiepenheuer & Witsch Verlag, Köln: 4

Landesbildstelle Berlin: 30, 51, 78, 104, 109, 129, 130, 178, 188, 194

Märkisches Museum / Stiftung Stadtmuseum, Berlin: 36, 92, 170

Ullstein Bilderdienst, Berlin: 70, 110, 152, 158, 206

Verlag Willmuth Arenhövel, Berlin: 151

Index

Page numbers in *italics* refer to illustrations.

ABOUT THE AUTHOR

Joseph Roth was born Moses Joseph Roth to Jewish parents on September 2, 1894, in Brody in Galicia, in the extreme east of the then Habsburg Empire; he died on May 27, 1939, in Paris. He never saw his father—who disappeared before he was born and later died insane—but grew up with his mother and her relatives. After completing school in Brody, he matriculated at the University of Lemberg (variously Lvov or Lviv), before transferring to the University of Vienna in 1914. He served for a year or two with the Austro-Hungarian Army on the Eastern Front—though possibly only as an army journalist or censor. Later he was to write: "My strongest experience was the War and the destruction of my fatherland, the only one I ever had, the Dual Monarchy of Austria-Hungary."

In 1918 he returned to Vienna, where he began writing for left-wing papers, occasionally as "Red Roth," "*der rote Roth.*" In 1920 he moved to Berlin, and in 1923 he began his distinguished association with the *Frankfurter Zeitung*. In the following years he traveled throughout Europe, filing copy for the *Frankfurter* from the south of France, the USSR, Albania, Germany, Poland, and Italy. He was one of the most distinguished and best-paid journalists of the period—being paid at the dream rate of one deutsche mark per line. Some of his pieces were collected under the title of one of them, *The Panopticum on Sunday* (1928), while some of his reportage from the Soviet Union went into *The Wandering Jews*. His gifts of style and perception could, on occasion, overwhelm his subjects, but he was a journalist of singular compassion. He observed and warned of the rising Nazi scene in Germany (Hitler actually appears by name in Roth's first novel, in 1923), and his 1926 visit to the USSR disabused him of most—but not quite all—of his sympathy for Communism.

When the Nazis took power in Germany in 1933, Roth immediately severed all his ties with the country. He lived in Paris—where he had been based for some years—but also in Amsterdam, Ostend, and the south of

France, and wrote for émigré publications. His royalist politics were mainly a mask for his pessimism; his last article was called "Goethe's Oak at Buchenwald." His final years were difficult; he moved from hotel to hotel, drinking heavily, worried about money and the future. What precipitated his final collapse was hearing the news that the playwright Ernst Toller had hanged himself in New York. An invitation from the American PEN Club (the organization that had brought Thomas Mann and many others to the States) was found among Roth's papers. It is tantalizing but ultimately impossible to imagine him taking ship to the New World, and continuing to live and to write: His world was the old one, and he'd used it all up.

Roth's fiction came into being alongside his journalism, and in the same way: at café tables, at odd hours and all hours, peripatetically, chaotically, charmedly. His first novel, *The Spider's Web*, was published in installments in 1923. There followed *Hotel Savoy* and *Rebellion* (both 1924), hard-hitting books about contemporary society and politics; then *Flight Without End*, *Zipper and His Father*, and *Right and Left* (all *Heimkehrerromane*—novels about soldiers returning home after the war). *Job* (1930) was his first book to draw considerably on his Jewish past in the East. *The Radetzky March* (1932) has the biggest scope of all his books and is commonly reckoned his masterpiece. There follow the books he wrote in exile, books with a stronger fabulist streak in them, full of melancholy beauty: *Tarabas, The Hundred Days, Confession of a Murderer, Weights and Measures, The Emperor's Tomb*, and *The Tale of the 1002nd Night*.

ABOUT THE TRANSLATOR

Michael Hofmann, the son of the German novelist Gert Hofmann, was born in 1957 in Freiburg. At the age of four, he moved to England, where he has lived off and on ever since. After studying English at Cambridge and comparative literature on his own, he moved to London in 1983. He has published poems and reviews widely in England and in the United States. In 1993, he was appointed Distinguished Lecturer in the English Department of the University of Florida at Gainesville.

To date, he has published four books of poems and a collection of criticism, *Behind the Lines*, all with Faber & Faber. He edited (with James Lasdun) a book of contemporary versions of the *Metamorphoses*, called *After Ovid*, and is editing *Rilke in English* for Penguin.

Hofmann has translated works by Bertolt Brecht, Franz Kafka, Wolfgang Koeppen, and Gert Hofmann, among others, and is the translator of the last six Joseph Roth titles to appear in English: *Right and Left*; *The Legend of the Holy Drinker*; *The Tale of the 1002nd Night*, for which he was awarded the PEN/Book-of-the-Month Club Prize for translation in 1998; *Rebellion*, for which he was awarded the Helen and Kurt Wolff Translation Prize in 2000; *The Wandering Jews*; and *The Collected Stories of Joseph Roth*.